Vintage Pellegrini

Vintage Pellegrini

The Collected Wisdom of an American Buongustaio

Writings by Angelo Pellegrini
Edited by Schuyler Ingle

SASQUATCH BOOKS
Seattle, Washington

Published by Sasquatch Books, 1931 Second Avenue, Seattle, Washington 98101

Library of Congress Cataloging-in-Publication Data

Pellegrini, Angelo M.
Vintage Pellegrini: the collected wisdom of an American buongustaio: writings/by Angelo
Pellegrini; edited by Schuyler Ingle.
p. cm.
ISBN 0-912365-45-5: $18.95.—ISBN 0-912365-44-7 (pbk.): $10.95
1. Italian Americans—Social life and customs. 2. Cookery. 3. Gardening.
4. Wine and wine making. 5. Pellegrini, Angelo M.
I. Ingle, Schuyler. II. Title.
E184.I8P43 1991
394.1'2'08951073—dc20   91-24127 CIP

Cover illustration by Murray Kimber
Cover design by Lynne Faulk
Interior design by Jane Jeszeck
Interior illustration by Patrick Howe

CREDITS
"The World I Left Behind," "The Initial Challenge," and "The Immigration of Mother and
Father" reprinted with permission of Macmillan Publishing Company from *Immigrant's Return*
by Angelo Pellegrini. Copyright ©1951, renewed ©1979 by Angelo M. Pellegrini.

"La Trombona," "Gathering Manure," "Father Dines with His Employer," "Toward
Humane Living," "A Slight Touch of Heresy," and "Meadowlarks" from *The Unprejudiced
Palate*, copyright ©1984 by Angelo Pellegrini. Published by North Point Press and reprinted
by permission.

"A World of Labor and Learning" from *American Dream* ©1986 by Angelo Pellegrini.
Published by North Point Press and reprinted by permission.

"La Bimbina" reprinted with permission of Macmillan Publishing Company from *Americans by
Choice* by Angelo M. Pellegrini. Copyright ©1956, renewed ©1984 by Angelo M. Pellegrini.

"Forty-Fifth Anniversary" first appeared in *The Seattle Times*.

"Why Garden?" and "Herbs" reprinted from *The Food Lover's Garden* by Angelo M. Pellegrini.
Copyright ©1970 by Angelo M. Pellegrini. Reprinted by permission of Alfred A. Knopf, Inc.

"The Mystique of Wine" and "Lean Years, Happy Years" reprinted with permission of
Madrona Publishing from *Lean Years, Happy Years* by Angelo Pellegrini. Copyright ©1973
by Angelo Pellegrini.

"Christmas in Italy," "Old Grand Dad," "Educating the Senses," "Soffritto," "Lamb,"
"Dandelion," "Artichoke," "Rabbit and Polenta," "Mushrooms," "Zucchini," "Risotto,"
"Tomatoes," and "Pelle's Folly" first appeared in *Seattle Weekly*.

"What Kind of People Would We Like to Be?" is from a speech given to the University of
Washington Medical Alumni Association in 1979 and first appeared in *University of Washington
Medicine*, Volume 7, Number 4, Winter 1980.

"My Father's Suspenders," "Angela in the Garden," and "Wine and Children" are from
Father and Son, an unpublished manuscript, ©1990 by Angelo Pellegrini.

CONTENTS

~~~~~

CONTENTS

V.

VI.

VII.

INTRODUCTION

I DROVE THROUGH McCleary recently, a small lumber town up in the clear-cut, reforested hills at the south end of Puget Sound that was the second boyhood home of Angelo Pellegrini. The old row houses, remnants of a once-thriving company town, have mostly given way to ranch-style ramblers and mobile homes. The old fruit trees blooming in the late northwestern spring spoke to the age of the town. Their trunks were massive, their bark craggy with age, their limbs twisted and distorted like old, arthritic fingers. Some of them must date back to the turn of the century, yet the unfolded petals at the tips of their new growth were as delicately colored and fresh as twilight.

Angelo Pellegrini is now as old and craggy as those fruit trees, some of which he may have planted, and each spring the sap flows in his veins with just as much promise. And some of it continues to spill out onto the printed page, a habit Pellegrini initiated with the publication in 1948 of *The Unprejudiced Palate*, a book about food and life that has the unique quality of remaining forever contemporary in spirit and message.

Coming to America early in the century from the Tuscan

hill town of Casabianca, Pellegrini settled in the Washington hill town of McCleary. There he made a successful transition from peasant boy to freedom-loving, anything-is-possible American youth, something he achieved without giving up his precious cultural identity to the melting pot. It is this quality of knowing what he has become as well as knowing where he has come from that he shares with his writings.

I first met Angelo Pellegrini when I interviewed him for a magazine assignment. We sat in his office in the English department at the University of Washington, where he was, by then, professor emeritus. The third-grade reading primer he had brought with him from Italy sat on a shelf above his desk. I had imagined we would talk about food and gardening, for such had been my intent. Our conversation, however, surged from the Italian Renaissance to Jeffersonian democracy to Shakespeare's sonnets to the American vision of Walt Whitman to the peculiar nature of primal fear in the peasant mind to the importance of the family and the time spent therein. And, of course, we talked about food and gardening and the baking of bread and the making of wine.

I subsequently wrote about Pellegrini as cook, gardener, author, winemaker, teacher, and mentor, and I heard back from more than one former student. "Dr. Pellegrini changed the course of my life with his lectures on Shakespeare," was a common theme in the letters. I could say much the same, though it wasn't his lectures on Shakespeare but his writings about food and gardening that captured my imagination. Food—the growing of it, the savoring of it, the preparation of it, the love of it —has often been Pellegrini's vehicle for driving home a message about the rich possibilities in a life lived close to its essentials, those of the body as well as those of the mind. By revealing the spirit with which he approached the spring garden or the dinner table or the wine cellar, he somehow gave me permission to borrow from his cultural heritage and call it my own, infusing my own heritage with new vigor. Angelo Pellegrini gave me a sense of tradition, and that gift appears to have changed the course of *my* life.

I met Angelo Pellegrini the second time in his kitchen. Like a poker player, I bought my way into the game with two plump rabbits culled from an abundance of young fryers in my backyard hutch. I had killed and cleaned them, and I handed them over at the door to Pellegrini's wife, Virginia, suggesting that she get them right into the refrigerator...as though Virginia wouldn't have known that. I walked back to my car muttering about what an idiot I must have seemed. But a dinner invitation followed. And dinner turned out to be an opportunity to watch and help Angelo Pellegrini cook.

Rabbit was the perfect dish for the occasion because it was rabbit that had given Angelo Pellegrini his first taste of culinary notoriety at the University of Washington. He was a student at the time. He writes about this in *The Unprejudiced Palate* (reprinted here on page 159), a dog-eared copy of which sticks out on my bookshelf. I knew about *soffritto*—a stew base created by finely mincing together a little onion, garlic, fresh herbs, celery, carrot, and pancetta, then gently sautéing that mass before adding meat and other ingredients—but I had no visceral experience of making a soffritto to call my own. Pellegrini gave me that, demonstrating that simply chopping wasn't enough, that one had to work in the fat of the pancetta, pounding it and smearing it with the side of a heavy knife, creating a singular unity, not a neat pile of separate ingredients. It takes time to make a soffritto, even, I have discovered, when the initial chopping is done with a food processor. It doesn't pay to rush.

There was more to this cooking experience than preparing a meal. While we stirred the pot, Pellegrini waved his long, sharp knife under my nose and told me that he had brought two things to his marriage: a good kitchen knife and a strong bed. Then, in a wavering croak of a voice, he sang for me the Italian ballad he had sung at night to Virginia many, many years before at the beginning of a successful courtship. He told me how to catch frogs and how to skin them and cook them with the herb *puleggio*, a cutting of which he gave me to plant at home; and he told me how his mother, when angry, would shake her fist and in a voice filled with maternal rage and love threaten to skin her recalcitrant children like frogs. He explained how he coaxed his own children into the love of food and wine, training their senses the way his father had trained his. With the radiant pride of an elder, he announced that his granddaughter had asked for her fifteenth birthday that she be allowed to come cook with him, her *Babbo*, and bring her friends. "Can you imagine?" he asked. And I could.

Angelo Pellegrini will tell you in the pages that follow of his childhood in Italy. He will tell you about coming to America, the land of possibility, and to Washington State. He will tell you about McCleary, where his active mind would seize on education as a springboard out of his past, where he had teachers wise enough to encourage him to melt a little for the melting pot, but just enough to get by, teachers who insisted that he keep hold of his language and his tradition. Their advice has paid off handsomely in what may be their best student. Now, those teachers reach through him and affect the rest of us.

I respond best to Angelo Pellegrini when he writes about food and gardening, but it would be a mistake to limit his appeal in this way. In writing about the immigrant experience, he speaks for all immigrants and the dignity of their struggle, whether they find themselves in their eighties or they are young and newly arrived and stumbling over the language, still full of hope for the future. He writes, as well, about our common past, about the people who cut the forests and built the railroads across the cleared land, and those who dug ditches from one end of the city to another. This place we call home, this Pacific Northwest, didn't just happen, and Pellegrini reminds us of the sweat and labor that have brought us this far.

I love Angelo Pellegrini for sharing his tradition. I am not unusual for having little or none of my own, my family having long since dissolved into the pot. I grow Tuscan cabbage from seed he gave me; I harvest and cook cardoons in much the same way he describes in *The Food Lover's Garden*. I husband my own small livestock for meat, but not so much out of my own tradition as in appreciation of the peasant tradition and way with food he taught me to respect. It is a tradition as honest as feast or famine. Pellegrini has given me a sense of my place on the earth, of life within the cycles of the earth, first through his writings and later through our modest friendship. I will forever honor him for this.

Schuyler Ingle
June 1991

9

THROUGH
A CHILD'S EYES

THE WORLD
I LEFT BEHIND

W HEN WE LEFT Italy, in the fall of 1913, I separated myself forever from a world to which I have frequently returned in memory. Many years later I was to realize that, to a child of nine years, immigration to America meant a new birth, to which a certain inevitable continuity with the past had given an added significance. The seven thousand miles which separates the state of Washington from Casabianca is the distance between two worlds fundamentally different. At this distance, and after having revisited my native land, I can state confidently that, for me, the distance was the interval between two births. It is no exaggeration to say that, in my childhood, I twice discovered life and the world; that, in fact, I have lived through two childhoods. The experience of an American child born, let us say, in Maine and transferred to California at the age of nine is in no way analogous.

May I allude briefly to the world I left behind, the world of a nine-year-old child, so many aspects of which I have never forgotten? What I shall have to say about that first world will be helpful toward an understanding of my reactions to the second.

I had been many years in America before I could see that world in perspective; before I could evaluate those early experiences, some of which I remembered so well. To be sure, it was the landscape of a poor child; but, even so, there was much in it which was utterly delightful. For I was born in the incomparable Tuscany countryside, in the vicinity of Florence, in the shadow of the Leaning Tower of Pisa, outside the medieval walls of Lucca, amid olive groves and vineyards. I remember particularly the early autumns, when the leaves were beginning to fall and the earth to harden with the early frosts. I remember walking barefooted to school, under the bright skies of Indian summer, quickening the pace to traverse more rapidly the shaded portions of the path, looking intently at the wayside vines for that last, possible cluster of grapes which had escaped the sharp eye of the gleaners. How precious, when found, that last sweet cluster! the final taste of the grape until the next season should come!

And I remember the winters! The long winter evenings I remember, with the family and the neighbors huddled at the hearth, with only the illusion of a fire to keep us warm; and how we took turns blowing in the coals to start a flame which soon thereafter subsided into thin ringlets of smoke. How the peasants unleashed their morbid imaginations and summoned forth horrible stories about the spirits of evil. The singing I remember; the passing of the wine jug; the final retreat into dark, cold, damp rooms, to sleep several in a bed, between sheets of homespun, rough, almost thorny, linen.

And the spring and early summer I remember! Like the hibernating animal, the peasant subsists during the barren winter months on his own substance. When spring comes he returns

again to the soil to gather the mushrooms, the tender shoots of
the turnip, the succulent core of the chicory; then to spade and
to rake and to sow, that later he may reap the fruit, the vegetables, the grain. I remember the anxiety with which we, sugar-
hungry peasants, awaited the first melons, the first fruit on the
tree, the first grape on the vine. Who, more acutely than the
peasant, is aware of the intimate, personal significance of the miracle of life? Rich, proud, centrally heated America, mark well my
word: you know not the agony of winter and the bliss of spring!
Some day, perhaps, when you may be old and shriveled and
exhausted, you will know their meaning. But today, you know
it not.

All these things I remember. They were the excitement and
the drama of my early years. But the experiences I remember
most vividly were even more intimately related to my life as a
peasant boy. I remember labor, unremitting toil, exalted in the
home, in the church, in the school, and its necessity quickly
realized by the growing child. I remember the stonecutters
crushing rock by hand for the roadbed; the women in the fields
hoeing, weeding, harvesting, and then rushing to the kitchen
to prepare dinner for the family; the men setting out with their
tools before the break of day; the bent grandmothers spinning,
weaving, and tending the children for their daughters; the draymen hauling rock, hay, and sand from sunrise to sunset; and
the venders, the beggars, the peddlers plying their trade in sun
and rain.

It is not an accident that after these many years I remember a certain picture in my second reader. It shows a group of
children seated around a table studying in the lamplight. The

caption reads: "Dopo il lavoro lo studio." (Study after the work is done.) Nor is it any more strange that the only story I remember in the same book had to do with Cecco, a lazy boy who was taken to an island by a strange little man on the assurance that there he would find a world of delicacies. When he arrived at the enchanted island, where fruit was growing in profusion, Cecco reached for an orange; but the orange burned his fingers and then lectured him in these words:

> *Alto là! Cecco sfacciato,*
> *A rubar chi t'ha insegnato?*
> *Se mangiarmi tu vorrai,*
> *Lavorar prima dovrai.*

(Hold on there, my brazen Cecco! Who taught you to steal? If you want to eat me, you must first *earn* the right to do so.)

Nor was I by any means a disinterested spectator of the laborious routine. I learned to work as I learned to walk. In bright-eyed, well-fed America, engrossed in devising community projects to keep the young out of mischief, where the strapping lad of sixteen must be bribed to mow the lawn, in America the vast playground, where everyone is either a playboy or an athlete, such things may seem incredible: but at the age of seven I worked for wages. I hired out as a human disk harrow, an adolescent clodbuster. Barefooted and in abbreviated breeches, I went to a neighbor's field to pulverize the clods of earth with a wooden mallet. All for a nickel a day! When I wasn't working as a hired hand I went forth in the summer sun as a rugged enterpriser to retrieve sand from the river. At convenient intervals on the steep bank I carved out ledges. Then I shoveled the sand from the riverbed onto the first ledge, from which I relayed it to the next, and on up to the top, where the drayman, to whom I sold it, could load it on his wagon and haul it away to the mason to whom he, in turn, sold it.

For a child under ten years of age, that kind of work was more than could be justified as wholesome discipline. It was discipline, I now realize; but in Casabianca the child worked as a matter of grim necessity. Among less arduous tasks, I remember particularly stripping leaves from the mulberry tree to feed the silkworms, and cutting grass, especially clover, to sell in small neat bundles to draymen along the highway. I went frequently to the main thoroughfare early in the morning with two or three dozen bundles of grass, to await the prospective buyers. During the autumn months I gathered fuel for the winter—any combustible remnants that could be found on a landscape where everyone was a gleaner and a scavenger. I also helped with the spading, the hoeing, the weeding, and—most pleasant of occupations—the harvest. On market days I followed the cattle and horses along the highway. For amusement? For diversion? Of course! A child must have his fun—even in Casabianca. But I pulled behind me a two-wheeled cart on which was strapped a huge basket—in case! And I kept my eyes fixed expectantly on the animals. When one of them hesitated in his jaunty strides, then humped his back and arched his tail, quick as a flash I was right there, shovel in hand. When the basket was full I retraced my steps to the stone cottage, as rugged and as proud and as confident as the president of the National Association of Manufacturers—though much less uncertain about the future.

Notwithstanding the constant labor, in which every member of the family participated, each according to his ability, I remember want—modest desires, humble yearnings, frequently immediate and vital needs, unfulfilled. There was always an abundance of such food; but our desire for meat, cheese, eggs, coffee, sweets, citrus fruit, and white bread was *never* satisfied. Except on rare occasions, and in microscopic quantities, we simply did not have them. Luxuries, I am leaving out of account, because we never pretended to have, nor even desired, what we knew a kind Providence had reserved for another class of people.

And I remember the awful distance that lay between us and what Silone has called the "citizens." In our village they were the doctor, the priest, the schoolmaster, the mayor, and their various brethren of the bourgeoisie. They expected and received from us obsequious acknowledgment of their superiority. They entered our world for favors; we entered theirs in service. One was expected to stand bareheaded in their presence and to address them only in the most formal terms. The relationship was accepted as a matter of course; it was only in retrospect, after I had been several years in America, that I realized there was something cruel and disgraceful about it.

Very early in life I learned that, except as masters, the chosen people were inaccessible to the poor. The haughty schoolmaster had a beautiful daughter—the only blonde in the community—with whom I had the misfortune to fall passionately in love at the ripe old age of eight. Her name, of course, was Beatrice. Because she was of the élite, she had a special seat in the schoolroom, by the side of her father's desk and facing the commoners.

Every day I found more and more irresistible the desire to

be close to my Love. With an instinct which only young lovers can understand, I found a way—a thorny, painful path, but a path which led to the feet of my Beloved. The standard punishment for behavior unbecoming a scholar, conceived with a certain diabolical finesse, was to make the villain kneel with bare knees on grains of corn scattered on the floor by the teacher's desk. One happy day, as I writhed and wriggled in the agony of unrequited love, I had an inspiration. I took my pen and jabbed it fiercely into the neck of the scholar who sat in front of me. The shrill, pitiful scream which followed, and which I had anticipated, brought me instantly to my feet. With more of pride than of sorrow I confessed my guilt—and, presto! I was kneeling at the feet of my Beloved. Thereafter, I became the most incorrigible brat in the schoolroom; but the schoolmaster's daughter, happily, was later wooed and won by someone else.

And I remember fear. Horrible memories of fear! At different times, in different places, different people fear different things; or certain species of fear are endemic to time, to place, and to culture.

Some of my fears as a child were of real, others of illusory, objects. But at the time they were all real to me; and the expression "We have nothing to fear but fear itself" would have left me simply bewildered in fear. I now realize that those fears were rooted in the culture. Among the real objects of my fear were the priest and the schoolmaster. I feared them because they were authoritarians who called the tunes, to which I could not always dance. They were the giants in a world of order and absolutes, with the privilege and the power to enforce their wills; while I was the dwarf whose inner necessities required a little anarchy and much flexibility in the precepts I was expected to follow. The schoolmaster operated with the rod, and invoked the law where he felt inadequate; the priest imposed the repetition of catechisms, and invoked the demons of hell and the wrath of God to allay recalcitrance.

I think I was a good rather than a bad boy. To be really bad requires time; and in the first world that I discovered I lacked the leisure indispensable to villainy. I don't remember ever having been severely punished; yet both my lay and my spiritual guides succeeded in making my life miserable. They were not exceptional in any way; they were simply the agents of time, place, and culture. I cringed under the threat they held over me. I remember the times, after having committed some horrible crime such as devouring a neighbor's apple, that I got to my knees and implored the Lord to forgive me, while I insisted that I had intended no harm. Perhaps it was my misfortune to have been born a rather decent creature. At any rate I lived in horror most of the time. I feared the two people whom in any decent society a child should love.

I know now that the most terrifying objects of my fear were illusory, although the culture insisted that they be accepted as real: witches, the devil with his three-pronged fork, serpents spawned in hell-fire, and the whole evil hierarchy of a cruel religious mythology. The atmosphere of the whole community was charged with real fear of the invisible world. It was sustained by gossip, by spectacle, by rites, and by myth. Shrines were set up in the fields and along the highways. Priests blessed vineyard and olive grove against the invisible enemy. Death was shrouded in a slimy mess of superstition. If the American funeral is too much a business transaction conducted in an atmosphere of piety and soft organ music, the Italian funeral was a transaction in piety conducted in an atmosphere of horror and garish symbolism. Its effect, whether intended or not, was to make the survivors strengthen their ties with the parish church.

The imagination of the community was morbidly preoccupied with witchery and the demons of darkness. There was a babe in the neighborhood who had been seriously ill for a long time. He was no more than two or three years of age. No one seemed to know what was wrong. I remember him in his crib, set near the threshold in the sun. He lay there, pale and motionless, day after day. I remember that his mouth was always open, that the flies buzzed over his face, entered into the mouth, the nostrils, and darted at his eyes. He never moved to protect himself.

When the peasants gathered at the hearth during the evening, they frequently speculated about the causes of the little tragedy. Of all the theories advanced, this has stuck in my mind: the child was bewitched. That had been "proved" by ripping open the mattress of his little crib, with the discovery that the feathers in it had been woven into intricate designs. It was, so the peasants concluded, the work of a witch who had entered the mattress and idled away the hours weaving feathers into patterns while she held the babe in her evil spell. That led to further speculation about the identity of the witch. Innuendoes were made about several people in the neighborhood, among them an old woman whom I loved, and a vicious crookback whom I feared and hated. I have forgotten what finally happened to the child.

But I remember tales about the crookback. He was a bad man and a tyrant, twisted into a knot perhaps by paralysis. He frequently passed the day in the local pub to which, since he could not walk, he was wheeled in a barrow by his wife, who was a fine woman, or by his daughter, who was a cruel wench and a match for an All-American fullback in strength. I remember him crouched in the barrow, growling and striking at his wife with a club, as she patiently wheeled him to his cronies at the pub. And I saw him one day giving the same treatment to his daughter—inadvisedly. For when she had had enough abuse she picked up the barrow and pitched father and all into the ditch.

It was the opinion of the community that crookback was a devil, in disguise. Which, of course, he was; but not in disguise. He was frequently held responsible and abused for community misfortunes. He was thought by some to be implicated in the babe's tragedy. Even my mother on one occasion accused him to his face of being the agent of evil. For some reason that I have forgotten—probably for plucking a cluster of grapes in crookback's vineyard—the savage daughter beat me severely, and I ran home in tears. Mother usually took the view that if someone flailed me I must have had it coming; but on that occasion both the extent of the beating and the administrator thereof enraged her. She took me by the hand and went to the crookback's house, where something awful which I have forgotten must have happened. But I remember Mother's parting thrust, delivered through clenched teeth and accompanied by a brandishing of the fist: "The good Lord has marked the agents of evil."

On another occasion—again as we were seated around the hearth in the evening—I listened to a strange tale told by a man who had some education and presumably should have known better. He told us that one night, a little past the midnight hour, as he was walking home along the top of the high riverbank he was attracted by a noise in the riverbed. Although he was terribly frightened he stopped to observe, and he saw three old hags splashing in the water. He yelled to them to get to their homes and to leave honest men like himself to walk the night in peace. When they did not move, but continued splashing, he fired several shots into their midst, and they disappeared.

After such tales as these I was expected to go upstairs to my bed and to sleep in blissful innocence. On the wall in my bedroom hung an ugly picture of hell with the devil presiding over the damned, and huge serpents gliding over the flames of burning brimstone. Is it any wonder that even as a grown child I had to be taken to bed by my mother, who stayed with me until I fell asleep?

I would not deal at such length with this experience of fear if it merely reflected a personal obsession. What I feared was what the community feared. Peasants regarded their superiors with awe and fear. The man who dared walk by the wall of a cemetery in the dark was a community hero. Fear is a way of life, rooted both in ignorance and in a keen sense of reality, and sustained in many parts of southern Europe by a clerical medievalism which time has not yet conquered. My children and the children of my neighbors, living in a different time, a different place, a different culture, know none of these fears.

—*Immigrant's Return*

LA TROMBONA

THEY WERE THE damndest pair that ever swore to be true to one another. He was a massive artisan, loose-jowled, grisly-bearded and sour faced. The hair on his broad, thick chest spilled over his shirt collar and curled in ringlets under his chin. Large rheumy tears flowed constantly from his big blue eyes, down along the deep channels between the heavy cheeks and bulbous nose, and mingled with the beads of sweat on his broad upper lip. The outer, hairy surface of his enormous hands, always powdered with a layer of fine sawdust, was crisscrossed with bulging blue veins.

As he wielded the broad ax on a knotted tree trunk or pushed the plane over the tough surface of an oak timber, he mumbled vigorously and incessantly such a streak of curses that mendicant friars who passed his shop habitually made the sign of the cross and repeated their *Pater Nosters* and *Ave Marias* with unwonted fervor. And yet, those who were not intimidated by his brusque exterior and stopped at his cottage never left empty-handed.

When he called to his wife, across the courtyard from his

24

workshop, to fetch him the wine jug, his affectionate love call was the envy of all hen-ridden males who lacked his gall, and the burly framework with which to back it up. *"Ei, brutta puttana sgangherata, quando me la porti quella benedetta bottiglia?"* What ho! You ugly, unhinged whore, when are you going to bring me that blessed bottle?

At the sound of her darling's voice, she emerged belligerently from the kitchen door, a mountainous, shapeless mass draped in a heavy, loose, and voluminous woolen dress that, so far as the neighbors could tell, had not been changed in a quarter of a century. It was gathered somewhere above the navel with a knitted bright red scarf and extended to the ground. As she waddled across the yard, her heavy breasts swaying rhythmically from side to side, she chewed incessantly on pumpkin seeds—of which she had an inexhaustible supply—and looked intently and rather menacingly toward the shop. When she approached her mate, whom she dearly loved, she held out the wine jug and addressed him in language as vigorous and original as his own. *"Ecco la tua puttana, brutto bastardo pidocchioso. Bevi e affoga, porco ghiottone."* Here comes your whore, you ugly, louse-ridden bastard. Drink and drown yourself, you gluttonous swine.

As she handed him the bottle, he hoisted his heavy-booted foot in the general direction of her belly. It was a wholly futile thrust, for she had learned by experience that by stooping slightly forward and grabbing his foot in mid-air, she could avoid his treacherous blow. When she had him thus helpless in her strong grip, she would grin and spit, then throw his boot to the ground and retreat, laughing like a witch. As she reached the middle of the courtyard she would turn her rear toward him, bend slightly forward, look over her shoulder and wink affectionately, as she let him have a blast so terrific that it fanned her skirt into a complete circle. Her talent for releasing such thunderclaps at will was so amazing that she was everywhere known as *la Trombona*.

In their rather unorthodox manner, they lived in perfect marital bliss. Power and will were so evenly divided between them that their amorous banter never resulted in harm to either one. They exemplified perfectly, though in a rather bizarre and exaggerated manner, the type of Latin man and wife who enjoy each other most, when each is yelling at the other and threatening in most forbidding language.

Although well past middle age, they had no children and lived alone in a stone cottage adjoining our home. Eating together at the hearth enormous quantities of good food washed down by goblets of wine was their principal recreation. He was a master craftsman, particularly skilled in shaping the trunk and root structure of oak and chestnut trees into magnificent plows. For his labor he was frequently paid in hams, sausages, eggs, poultry, wine, and grain. Thus, and since they had no dependents, they could afford to live well above the level of the peasants whom he served in a hundred different ways.

If the reader will search his memory, he may likely discover that in his childhood there was some adult, outside of the home, who was his dearest friend; some kindly elder, full of affection and patience, who knew how to make children happy. In my childhood and early youth there were several, but none so dear as *la Trombona* and her mumbling husband. Frequently, in the morning, they called me in to share their breakfast of toasted bread dunked in large bowls of coffee and milk nicely sweetened with priceless sugar and spiked with *acquavite*. Now and then they would fry me an egg or give me a slice of ham to eat with my figs and bread. He was never too busy to help me make a kite or construct a little wagon for my manuring expeditions.

Occasionally, when he delivered a finished plow, he took me with him to the country. When the donkey was hitched to the wagon, he put me in the driver's seat and let me hold the reins as he walked alongside the animal. One such expedition, to a particularly distant farmhouse, ended most tragically. The farmer had given us dinner, a load of hay, and a precious ham in payment for the plow. Because of the load and the difficult terrain, we were obliged to walk most of the way home and occasionally to give the donkey a hand over a rut or up a difficult incline. But it was late at night and I was soon tired and sleepy; so I was hoisted on top of the hay and given the responsibility of guarding the ham against possible loss as we jogged along over the uneven roadbed. When we arrived home about midnight, *la Trombona* was waiting for us with hot coffee and fresh bread, eager to sample the new ham. But the ham had been lost. The fury and the noise of the quarrel which ensued still ring in my ears. Although, in a way, I had been principally at fault, no harsh word was spoken to me. They abused and threatened each other until the good man, with lantern in hand, retraced his steps in search of the ham. I don't remember whether it was ever found.

—*The Unprejudiced Palate*

CHRISTMAS
IN ITALY

"To bed! To bed! Or else..." Thus said my mother to me and my younger brother one evening years ago in Italy. "You heard what Mother said. Now come along, quickly!" And thus our sister, who by virtue of being fifteen, about twice our age and the eldest child, served as Mother's lieutenant in supervising the conduct of the rest of us. But my brother and I groaned disapproval. "Can't we stay up a little longer?"

The time was winter. It was bitter cold outside and no less cold in the unheated bedroom upstairs. An uncle and an aunt had joined us after dinner. Having roasted and eaten chestnuts, we were now in a semicircle in front of the fireplace. Uncle Narciso had just told us a scary fairy story in the dim light of the embers of a spent faggot. A fresh one was tossed on the live coals. It crackled and blazed brilliantly in a burst of flame. In its light, my brother and I could see our long woolen stockings hanging at opposite ends of the mantle.

A faggot is a bundle of sticks, mostly prunings and trimmings from vines and trees. It was our principal kind of fuel for cooking and heating. My brother and I had gathered a good number of these during the fall months, with the understanding that more would be burned on this evening than at any other time. We had done what was required of us to make this possible and to add to the winter's supply of fuel. We felt comfortable about this, glowed a little with self-importance in the light of our blazing faggot; and once again we petitioned authority, "May we stay up a little longer? Roast a few more chestnuts? Have another story?"

This time the answer to our petition was a spine-chilling *hee-haw, hee-haw, hee-haw,* which came to us from the bitter cold outside. She had arrived earlier than expected! La Befana was approaching the door! As if in flight from a wolf, my brother and I bounded up the stairs and got into bed.

Who was la Befana? She was to Italian children what Santa Claus is to American children. The Befana myth derives from the Epiphany, also called Twelfth Night, a yearly festival in many Christian churches held on January 6 to commemorate the coming of the Three Wise Men to the infant Jesus. From this clerical origin, the transition to the secular tradition was a commendable progression; for as the Wise Men bore gifts to the infant Jesus, manifesting his divinity, la Befana comes bearing gifts to children who are worthy of them and thus manifests their virtue. The tradition, expounded by parents to their children, amounts to this: in order to be rewarded by la Befana you must have been a good child. It is understood, of course, that they shall decide what the word "good" means.

La Befana is an old and ugly witchlike hag. Since I have never seen her, my knowledge of her is no more than I acquired in that tiny community in Italy, known as Casabianca, where I was born and raised to the age of ten. She is very severe, loves industrious children and loathes lazy ones. I still remember the Italian for this: *ama i bimbi laboriosi e disprezza quelli oziosi*. She comes astride a donkey in the middle of the night preceding January 6. She will not stop at homes where children are not in bed. She is chilled to the bone no matter what the weather, and must be thawed out, so to speak, when she enters a home so that she may be able to make it to the next. Hence the need for extra wood to burn on the eve of January 6. Where there is no wood, no gifts are left.

This chill factor in the Befana myth may have been invented by the wise old peasants in and around Casabianca, where fuel was scarce, in order to provide an incentive for children to scrounge the countryside for fuel, especially after the pruning season. Whether it was a part of the myth elsewhere, I do not know; that it was central to it among the poor in the little and only world I knew as a young boy, there is no doubt. Nor is there any doubt that it was used with telling effect to make us children ingenious gleaners and scroungers.

In that little world, a good boy or girl was an industrious one. We may also have been obedient, kind, respectful, mannerly; but, though desirable, these were "frill virtues." The central and definitive attribute was an enduring willingness to labor, for every child to do his or her utmost toward the support of the family. This imperative was driven home to us by parents, teachers, and priest. Had I been asked, "What is the purpose of life?" —a question that philosophers have never agreed on—my answer would have been prompt and certain: "Work is the purpose of life. Man was created so that he might discover how difficult it is to survive."

The meaning of being good as a central virtue changed with the seasons in the peasant world, where dependence on the land for the daily bread was total. When we children were able to walk, when we had learned how to use the peasant's tools and were beginning to realize that we must earn our bread by the sweat of our brow, we were being good when we labored as we could and as each season required. And, in preparation for la Befana and the Epiphany, the autumn required fuel to keep the home fires burning and to warm the cockles of la Befana's heart.

We had been good boys. In the bright glow of one of those burning faggots we had seen our long, woolen stockings. We had heard the *hee-haw* of the Befana's donkey—never mind how it was contrived—and we had gone dutifully to bed. What would be our reward? We would know in the morning.

It was modest but immensely satisfying. No toys—there would have been no time to play with them anyway. There was a foot-long pinecone filled with pine nuts, an orange, some filberts, chestnuts, and walnuts, a lump of sugar. That was all—all edibles!

I have written the above so that it may be read on the first day of winter and two days before Santa Claus comes to the children of a land I thought of as an earthly paradise of abundance when I first came to it seventy years ago. It is less so now, and it will be even less so tomorrow. In preparing children for Santa Claus, let us bear in mind the ethic of the la Befana myth as it relates to the current global problem of depleting resources; let us warn them that Santa rewards only those who have been good, in the sense defined above—those children who have been productive by avoiding waste and by careful husbandry of all their possessions. By this commendable strategy, we will enlist the aid of the children in making the conservation of resources the community's collective response to the lean years. Utopian? Not at all. Children can and are willing to learn if they are properly taught. The responsibility is ours; their performance is the measure of our trust in them.

—*Seattle Weekly*

GATHERING MANURE

"THREE YARDS OF manure. Well! You are going to America. Well! And you are leaving tomorrow afternoon. Well!" He took a handful, felt its texture between the finger tips, raised it to the nostrils. "Young man, you have polluted this with fillers. I can still smell the hay and the straw. But since you are going far away, never to return, I'll be generous with you. How about thirty-five cents?"

He was a shrewd peasant and I a shrewd lad. We both knew that notwithstanding the straw and the hay in it, the manure was worth a dollar. But he had me on the hip, and so I was obliged to liquidate my assets at a sacrifice before leaving for my new home, one-fourth the distance around the world.

He was right. I had mixed considerable hay and straw with the cow pats and horse dumplings; but since my original plan had been to sell the manure the following spring, by which time the fillers would have been completely rotted, my conduct had not been entirely dishonorable. It was just my tough luck that I had to sell before my scheme had thoroughly ripened.

The proper inference from this is that I was skilled in the techniques of free enterprise long before I had been told that it is synonymous with The American Way of Life. So much so, indeed, that I might say I was Americanized before I had even thought of coming to America. Furthermore, I had the makings of a solid American on other grounds. My origins were no less humble than Lincoln's. He got his start in life splitting rails; I got mine gathering manure on the highway. He went on to become our most distinguished president, the Great Liberator, the author of the Gettysburg Address. From gathering manure I went on to America, to a new way of life, to teaching eager youth. The parallel is not wholly facetious.

But let me go back to my free-enterprising childhood that I may explain how, on the eve of my departure for the New World, I had accumulated assets liquidated at thirty-five cents. As befits an enterpriser of heroic caliber, I always had several projects under way; but gathering manure was the most exciting, if not the most profitable. Moreover, it was highly competitive —not simply in theory, but in fact. There were no secret agreements among the gleaners of manure, no hidden combines plying their trade behind the facade of a plausible formula. The competitors worked shoulder to shoulder in an undertaking that afforded excellent opportunity for the development of shrewdness, an attribute central in all business success.

On Wednesdays and Saturdays the peasants drove their livestock to market for barter, sale, or exchange. Early in the morning on these days, we children of the neighborhood went to the highway with shovels and hand-drawn carts to await the driven animals—cows, horses, mules, sheep, and goats. For obvious reasons we preferred the larger animals, and when a goodly number came by, we shadowed their tails.

In all competitive undertakings there are rules and regulations, and we had our own. It is axiomatic, of course, that cow pats and horse dumplings cannot be gathered, even by the most zealous enterpriser, until the animals see fit to release them. When the release occurred, it presented a problem: who, of the twelve or so gleaners, was to have them? If all rushed for the booty in a mad scramble, the likely result would have been broken skulls and almost certainly total waste of the product. We had had no course in economics to guide us, but I think our disposition of the problem was entirely fair. When the animals came by, each lad chose the one—or more, depending on the size of the herd—he thought would most likely relieve himself within a reasonable time. There were empirical grounds on which the choice could be made, as I suppose there are objective data to guide one who dabbles in stocks and bonds. And, of course, the shrewd lad who knew best the intimate habits of horses and cattle always came out on top of the heap.

One could tell, for example, by a careful examination of the rump, tail, and legs of the animal, whether he had recently relieved himself of yesterday's hay. Under the circumstances, unfortunately, the test was not always reliable, since the peasants were also shrewd and kept their cattle clean for the market. Furthermore, in anticipation of market day, some of the animals had been fed grain and hay rather than grass, a diet that normally results in solid evacuation, neatly deposited and with no telltale traces.

The shrewd manure gatherer knew also that cows and horses frequently give certain premonitory signs before they do the deed. There is a perceptible hesitation in the jaunty stride, a slight hunching of the back, a characteristic restlessness in the tail, and successive dilations and contractions in the visible part of the organ involved. Unfortunately, these signs were not always reliable, since on occasion they turned out to be overelaborate preambles to an absolutely noncollectable puff of wind. However, an animal who went through such maneuvers, we all knew, bore diligent watching.

The clever boys—and I was one of them—supplemented these observations with such an intuitive grasp of the whole situation as cannot be described. When, as frequently happened, several of us chose to shadow the same tail, we had recourse to the drawing of straws. Now and then the winner who, as it turned out, had picked a dud, came in for considerable ribbing.

Thus we wove in and out of the animal ranks, scampering ahead or darting behind, to follow new herds when we were satisfied that the one just shadowed had given all that could be reasonably expected. As the last animals passed on their way to market, we raced home to prepare for school. The most resourceful among us dragged a rake behind the cart and thus picked up bits of hay and straw that had shaken loose from the draymen's wagons. These were added to the morning's haul to increase its bulk. The manure was then piled in the barnyard to be sold in the spring—for profit. Where could one find a better example of free enterprise and fair enterprisers?

When I arrived in America and settled in a small town in the Northwest, I soon discovered that my manure-gathering days were over; indeed, that my whole attitude toward the subject would have to be fundamentally revised.

I had heard about freedom in America. To me it had meant simply the absence of confinement, such as being tied to the bed-post when Mother had to go to the fields; and that happened only when I was a tiny tot just learning to walk into mischief. For the rest, I had enjoyed too much freedom, scouring the countryside in search of subsistence. And confinement I had always associated with a necessary restriction on animals. Where I lived, land was precious and grazing unknown. We had cut the grass, trimmed the vine and corn tassels, stripped the leaves from certain trees, and served our animals all their meals in bed, so to speak.

When I discovered that in America freedom is extended to cattle and horses, I was no little amazed. It took a little while to realize that the ding-dong of the cowbell was not in reality an ambulatory campanile. The cow was literally ubiquitous, and wherever she grazed, frequently not a dozen paces from the front door, she left the acrid, steaming token of gratitude. It thus became obvious that my offensive strategy was no longer necessary; so I passed to the defensive phase of operations and began to ponder the means for keeping both the cow and her generous gifts out of the parlor. Phenomenal America, I thought, as I added manure to my blessings, is there no end to your prodigality?

—*The Unprejudiced Palate*

A WORLD OF
LABOR AND
LEARNING

WHEN FATHER SUMMONED us to join him and gave an account of the resources he had found in McCleary, he said nothing about educational opportunities for us children. When, after our arrival, he took us on a tour of the landscape that would be our home, noting several times with the pride of a benefactor that all we saw was essentially our own, he did not direct our attention to the schoolhouse, plainly visible on a hill at the edge of the forest. Why the omission?

There are two reasons. We had come to America in search of bread, and not of anything else implied in the word "opportunity." The word, so current in the American way of life, was not in the vocabulary of the peasant; the options to which it referred were unknown in his world. Furthermore, in our heritage there was no tradition of culture as formal education. Father had one year of formal education; mother had none. Since education had not been their expectation, they did not particularly

38

regret the lack of it. For these reasons father had not directed our attention to the schoolhouse, and none of us had really noticed the omission.

Had father known what his firstborn son would eventually learn, he would have realized that the school was a part of the structure and plan of the new land and a central element in its pragmatic philosophy. America, with its commerce and industry expanding on the eve of World War I, needed educated workers. Thus, when we arrived on the scene, the concept of education for all, gratis for the lower grades and at a minimum cost in college, was already current in American society. It was uniquely American. Had father known this, he would have realized that an adequate appraisal of the new land's resources must include education for the children, that there could be no way of avoiding the little school at the top of the hill.

The new land was strange in many ways; the strangest of these was that it required children to go to school until they were sixteen years of age. We were informed of this fact by the principal of the McCleary school. He came into our home as one who bears good news, not in the least aware that we might find it incomprehensible. There are two laws, he told us: Children must attend school until they are sixteen or have completed the eighth grade; and their employment in industry is prohibited until they reach that age. He welcomed us warmly into the community, and told us that the teachers were excellent and anxious to help us in all possible ways.

So that was the law! Incredible! Father reacted to its requirement with his habitual prudence. He granted that such a law might seem strange and absurd, but, he noted, there was no alternative but obedience. What he privately thought, not so much about the merits of the law as about his firstborn son going to school for another six years, I never did know. The merits of educational policy were not discussed in a peasant's home. However, we were ancestrally conditioned to obedience to authority, so what the state required, wisely or otherwise, must be obeyed. What would be my father's attitude toward my continuing school beyond what the law required? Would he readily agree to my going to the university in the big city, miles and miles away? When I returned to school in January 1914, this question was not yet within the range of our imagination. However, in a few years I would press the issue, and father would have to commit himself.

When I began a new life in this blessed land of labor and learning, my parents planned the daily labor. There was much to do in order to maintain and add to the standard of living we had achieved by the end of the first year. Land to cultivate, animals to tend to, fuel for the wood-burning stove to cut and fetch home from the forest; it was all labor that we were skilled in and did with a certain zest because it was immediately remunerative in a way and a degree hitherto unknown to us. It made us rich in the basics of life.

The kind destiny that attended my nativity provided me with a succession of wise, affectionate teachers of archetypal competence. In the world of learning, these would be my surrogate parents and would affect the course of my education. Within six months, the first of these had taught me enough of the English language so that I could enter the fourth grade, where I properly belonged at ten years of age. She immediately accepted the challenge I posed: I was a young boy willing to learn who must learn the language as quickly as possible. To that end, she devised an inspired strategy.

She explained it to me about fifty years later, when I discovered her quite by chance in a retirement home. Her name was Ivah Dobbs. She taught the first four grades. According to her plan, the first-grade children would actually do the preliminary teaching, and I would learn to read precisely as they had learned at the start of the school term. (I joined the class three months after the start of the year.)

This is what she told me: "You were a strange appearance in our schoolroom and the center of attention for the first few days. You were dark and they were blond. The clothes you wore were unlike theirs. Since you knew no word of English, you never spoke. When someone asked your name, you shrugged your shoulders. You were a few years older than they and you never smiled. So I told them your name and something of what they should know about you in order to make them comfortable in your presence. This relieved them of their anxiety and made them eager to assist me in teaching you the language."

Her plan was flawless and produced immediate results. She told the class that for my benefit they would repeat the beginning reading exercises. The first-grade reader was actually a book of drawings and pictures and, written in large letters under each, was the identifying legend. Thus on page one was the picture of a dog, and under it was the simple declarative, "This is a dog." There followed other pictures similarly identified. Standing in front of the class with reader in hand, each child in turn would read aloud, clearly and slowly, beginning on page one. The teacher would sit by me and point with her finger at each word as it was pronounced. Some of the words she pronounced herself, showing me how to produce the sound by proper placement of the lips and tongue.

The first to read for me was a little lad whose hair was parted in the middle. His complexion was the fairest of the fair, his face was narrow, and his mouth small with lips slightly pursed, but his voice was strong and he read well. Holding the reader firmly in both hands, he stood before the class looking intently at the page, anxious, no doubt, to avoid making a mistake in his first performance as a teacher. When he felt sure of himself, he raised his head, looked straight at me and pronounced the historic declarative, "This is a dog." The teacher, showing me how to pronounce the, to me, unfamiliar "th" sound, repeated, "This is a dog." And I understood every single word! In my great excitement, the built-in frown vanished and I smiled.

Putting words and pictures together, I immediately inferred the meaning of the brief declarative and translated it into Italian: *Questo è un cane.* The same number of words. "This is a dog" must mean *Questo è un cane.* Making similar inferences, I translated other simple declaratives read to me. Thus by the end of that day I knew for certain the English pronoun "this," the indefinite article "a," the verb "is," and the nouns "dog," "cat," "rat," "boy," "girl." In the same manner, during the next few days, I learned the indefinite article "an," the definite article "the," and other nouns. From this sound beginning I quickly progressed to other forms: "these," "that," "those," "am," "are."

In learning so much that was fundamental in so little time,

my knowledge of Italian was a considerable aid. Here I must make a relevant observation. The study discipline in an Italian school was imposed without mercy, especially in reading, writing, and arithmetic. No time was lost in pleasant diversions such as I found in the American schoolroom. The pace was swift, the standards high. Those who could not keep abreast were left behind. The Darwinian hypothesis was at work in the classroom. The practical result was that a graduate of the third grade knew as much about reading, writing, and arithmetic as a sixth-grader in the American school. Being such a graduate, I knew what my little teachers did not know—the elements of grammar and sentence structure. Since these are essentially similar in the two languages, my knowledge of Italian greatly facilitated my learning to read and write English. But learning to speak the language, to articulate it as a native, was more difficult. There were sounds, such as "th," that were unfamiliar. It would take time to learn to produce such sounds perfectly. And then there were words such as "tough" and "dough" that one simply had to accept on faith.

Thus, after one week of such exercises that the teacher devised, what had been completely dark was now clear. I no longer despaired. I felt confident that I would soon know the written language as well as my peers. What a relief to know that the language could be learned! What a thrill to hear "This is a dog" and understand what was heard ! How exciting to cease being totally dumb! O this learning, what a thing it is!

And here I must give due credit to the teacher. She was as determined as I that I should learn the language in the shortest possible time. She became my friend, my tutor, and my guide.

Had she been unsympathetic, or less skilled, I should have fared differently. She worked with me during the recess period, the lunch hour, and after school. She brought me into her home and, relentlessly pursuing the same method—"this is a chair," "this is a table," "that is the floor"—she enlarged my vocabulary and gradually taught me to see, to hear, to think, and to articulate in English. She drilled me in the elements of English grammar, especially in the conjugation of basic verbs, and after each session with her I religiously practiced what I had learned. Given her skill and devotion as a teacher and my own determination and self-discipline, at the end of six months in school I had learned enough of the language to be advanced to the fourth grade.

While thus learning the language, I continued to be an amused and fascinated spectator. Here I make no claim to having had an acuteness of observation beyond my years. During the time that I was effecting a transition from the Old to the New World, there were certain comparisons that even one so young as I could not fail to note. Between McCleary and Casabianca there was a dramatic difference in what I may call the ethics, conventions, and code of behavior that prevailed in the school. In the one, the necessary discipline was tempered by friendliness and informality; in the other, it was aggravated by the severe formality of the guardhouse. The code was sensibly permissive in the one, rigidly authoritarian in the other. When the teacher entered the schoolroom in Casabianca, the students stood at attention by their benches and sat when ordered to do so; the least infraction of the code was severely punished.

Here it was altogether different. The teacher was at her desk when the young ones drifted into the room. She greeted each one by name, caressed them, asked questions, commented on their apparel, graciously accepted what little gifts the students might offer, usually fruit or a flower. And the little ones themselves approached the teacher each morning as they would a doting grandmother. There was no cleavage between pupil and teacher, and unbecoming behavior was gently reprimanded: "Now Johnny, you mustn't pull Betty's hair! You wouldn't want someone to do that to you, would you?"

I noted in the classroom what I had also observed among the people in the town, namely that there were no visible class distinctions. No one appeared privileged, the teacher dealt with each one with amiable impartiality. The children of the McCleary brothers and of the company executives were in that school, but it was not possible to distinguish them from those of the loggers and mill hands. They all dressed pretty much alike and mingled freely. (In Casabianca, the daughter of the schoolteacher had, so to speak, a reserved seat in the room. Since she had caused certain amorous stirrings in me, I wrote her a letter from McCleary. She did not reply. My impertinence in writing to her must have offended her.)

There was also a marked difference in the general approach to education. As I have already noted, the study discipline in Casabianca was imposed without mercy. It was all work and no play. In McCleary the learning process was casual and relaxed. Work and play were nicely balanced so that the transition from the one to the other was scarcely noticed. The day was begun with a singing session—a strange though pleasant way to begin the school day! Each day the teacher read a short story or an episode of a long one to the class. There were mid-morning and mid-afternoon recesses and friendly competitions in spelling and arithmetic. There were reports on activities—who had an interesting experience to share with the class? The intent seemed to be to make the day at school as pleasant as possible.

I had known none of these amenities in the school in Casabianca. In the third grade we had begun the day with a rigorous exercise in composition. The teacher chose the subject and she required from each pupil, with no questions permitted, an acceptable essay on any phase of the subject. She accepted nothing short of perfection, nor was she unique in this requirement. The principal emphasis in the Italian school was on mastery of the language, Dante's *dolce stil nuovo*; the language that had so fascinated a great English poet that he had referred to it as:

That soft bastard Latin
Which melts like kisses from a female mouth
And sounds as if it should be writ on satin.

Granted! The teacher's objective was commendable, but to require children of peasants who had no cultural heritage whatever to do justice to such a language in a daily composition was to impose on them a duty that made them sweat with the fear of failure. I myself had done rather well in such exercises, but I must confess that beginning the day with a burst of song was much more fun.

—*American Dream*

My
Parents

FATHER DINES
WITH HIS
EMPLOYER

IT WAS MY father's first dinner at the home of his employer, a wealthy French merchant in Marseilles—and his first
experience at an aristocrat's dinner table. He was understandably
nervous, for in such an environment he was uncertain of his
behavior. The vermouth *apéritif* had been served and dispatched
with no difficulty. Father knew well enough how to drink even
in the most elegant company. Nor had the appetizers and soup
posed any perplexing problem in etiquette. But when the main
course was brought to the table, Father was visibly shaken. He
was served an individual casserole containing a neatly quartered
quail, barely visible in a sauce that immediately sought and found
the nostrils of a peasant who knew his bread and wine. The issue
was clear-cut: what were the permissible means, at an aristocrat's
table, for getting that sauce to the stomach?

Father was a man who never compromised on food and
drink. He was an enlightened peasant gourmet with a remarkable

49

catholicity of taste and an instinctive appreciation of all that is good to eat and drink. Within the confining orbit of a peasant's means, he sought to live a humane life. Even in his work, among the peasants in Tuscany, in the vineyards of Algiers, and in the lumber camps of our own Northwest, he enjoyed the reputation of one who did even the most menial tasks with distinction. The achievement of quality was his preoccupation in everything to which he set his capable hands.

At the dinner table he was really not difficult to please. He enjoyed audibly the simplest fare so long as it had been prepared with reasonable care. Frequently he dined happily on soup, bread, cheese, and fruit; but he insisted that each of these ingredients in the evening meal be the best possible under the circumstances. He could never forgive an unsuccessful loaf of bread, for his standard of achievement completely excluded the possibility of failure in such matters. Nor, for the same reason, could he gracefully pardon Mother for an occasional slip in an otherwise faultless cuisine.

His reaction to food was always unambiguous. An excellent soup, a delicious roast, his favorite vegetable from the garden, would always lift him from a dark mood and unlock his tongue. As he drew his chair to the table, he could tell from the fragrance the quality of what he was about to eat; and when he was pleased by the promise of a good dinner, he became the most infectiously happy man that ever wielded knife and fork. His good humor, released in gaiety, tall stories, and happy banter, completely dominated the dinner hour. He was a joy to everyone who watched him as he sucked the bones and ground the more tender ones with his hard white teeth to extract the marrow. His ability to clean a bone and lick the platter clean, always performed with refinement and skill, I have never seen equaled.

His only praise of a dinner that pleased him thoroughly was implicit in the mood that it evoked and the manner in which he gave it to his stomach. Nor did he complain when the fare fell short of his exacting standards. Mother's most frequent aberrations in the kitchen were always explainable in terms of a demoniacal tendency to oversalt. She frequently confessed that when she shook the salt cellar over a dish, an evil power, bent on ruining the home, took possession of her. The consequence was that too often a good soup was ruined by too much salt. But Father was too much the gentleman to make a fuss on such occasions. When he discovered that any part of the dinner had received a reckless benediction of sodium chloride, he became a dark, threatening cloud. His swarthy complexion literally darkened, and without as much as grunting a word of disapprobation, he went to the kitchen sink, spilled the contents of his dish and, with ceremonious care, fried himself two eggs and returned to the table. No one in the family heard him utter a word until the next dinner— which, you may be sure, was always good. Men who grumble and growl and swear when a housewife fouls up a recipe should reflect on my father's behavior and look to their manners.

Well! this peasant gourmet found himself, at the age of thirty-five and after the birth of his third of six children, in the service of M. Charbonnier of Marseilles, France. It was an employment that he had secured through his shrewd and resourceful wife and eminently suited to his temperament, his talents, and his flair for distinguished cuisine.

M. Charbonnier had extensive vineyards in Algiers. My father was employed as general supervisor of the vineyard and

FATHER DINES WITH HIS EMPLOYER

wine making. His duties entailed frequent visits to his employer's home in Marseilles. Immediately before the vintage he had to consult with his chief about the wines that were to be made. That involved an inventory of the Charbonnier cellar to determine the needs, and a general report on what the vineyard might be expected to yield. When the vintage was completed and the various wines were tucked away in storage cooperage, Father was again expected to cross the Mediterranean for a general report to his employer. In addition to these two visits, there were to be as many others as the competent performance of important duties made necessary.

This pleasant employment lasted from 1906 to 1911, when it was brought to an end by the Italo-Turkish war, September 29, 1911. During the five years that Father was in the service of M. Charbonnier, he lived the life of Riley. He loved his work, to which he brought unusual talents, and he came to love his employer, who was by any standards a Man. After the first year his visits to the Charbonnier residence became primarily excursions into friendship and good food. The war with Turkey called him back to Italy and soon thereafter sent him back to Africa in a corporal's uniform. But this story has to do with his initial dinner at the Charbonnier table.

What were the permissible means, at an aristocrat's table, for getting that sauce to the stomach? Father did some fast thinking. He eliminated the method of sopping it up with his bread, which he could do with extraordinary skill, because he thought that might make a bad impression on his employer and so place his new position in jeopardy. It then occurred to him that he might wait and follow safely the example of his host. But that course

MY PARENTS

of action he dismissed, too, as utterly unsatisfactory. Charbonnier might be the exceptional Frenchman who did not appreciate a good sauce—or he might unduly delay the ingestion until the sauce was cold and therefore unfit to eat. What to do? A glass of Burgundy brought immediate inspiration.

"Monsieur Charbonnier," said my father, "have you ever been told how the Leaning Tower of Pisa was built?" "No," said his host, somewhat startled by a question so completely irrelevant. "Well, it isn't such a mystery as some would have us think," continued my father, visibly haunted by the fumes of the tantalizing sauce. "You know, of course, that the tower is round." As he said this, he took a piece of bread, described a complete circle in the casserole, and stuffed the bread quickly into his mouth. "Oh yes, *completely* round," he added as he repeated the gesture. "Some people can't understand why it leans on one side." He proceeded with some difficulty, as his mouth was crammed to capacity and he was trying to swallow as fast as he thought consistent with good manners. "From an engineering point of view, the explanation is simple. Any structure can be made to lean in any direction by the simple expedient of sinking the foundation a little deeper on the side where the slant is desired. For example, if I want the tower to lean toward me, I make the foundation deeper on this side," he said triumphantly as he hammered in rapid succession with a piece of bread the appropriate spot in the casserole. "If I want it to lean toward you, I dig deeper on that side." And he repeated the lively illustration.

"Once the foundation has been dug, the rest is simple. The stones are then set in place, round and round and round, always following the established contour, until the desired height is reached." By this time, several slices of bread had been consumed and there were only a few traces of sauce left in the casserole. With success within his grasp, he continued confidently. "When the desired altitude has been attained, all that remains is to super-impose a guard rail all around, and behold! the Leaning Tower of Pisa." The last circular swipe removed all traces of sauce from the casserole.

M. Charbonnier, with an understanding smile and the dev-il's twinkle in his eyes, looked at my father and said, "Marvelous!" He then raised his casserole to his lips, took the sauce in two experienced gulps, and burst into a belly laugh that was period-ically renewed thereafter as frequently as the two men met. And that was the beginning of a friendship that, but for the intrusion of Italy's imperial ambitions, might have endured unto death.

—*The Unprejudiced Palate*

The Immigration
of Mother
and Father

THE TRACING OF events to their causes frequently in-
volves oversimplification. I recognize and accept this risk when
I say it is not likely that I would be here now, writing this story
in my study on View Ridge, if my father had not met Swan
Sistrom, a burly, amiable Scandinavian, somewhere in the state
of Washington early in 1913. How they met, I have never
known; but that Sistrom persuaded Father to send to Italy for his
wife and children is an established fact.

In 1912 we were a family of seven in Casabianca, a small
community a few miles west of Florence, where we worked a
bit of land as sharecroppers. The children, of whom I was the
third, ranged in age from two to fourteen years. The central,
dominating fact of our existence was continuous, inadequately
rewarded labor. It was not possible then, and is much less now,
for a peasant to make an adequate living in Italy without own-
ing his home and a few acres of land.

Education beyond the third grade was out of the question. The overwhelming majority of literate Italian immigrants in America would tell you, should you ask them, that they quit school after the third grade. It is not a matter of a magic number. At eight or nine years of age, if not sooner, the peasant child is old enough to bend his neck to the yoke and to fix his eyes upon the soil in which he must grub for bread. I did not know it then, but I know it now, that it is a cruel, man-made destiny from which there is yet no immediate hope of escape.

Father and Mother were an excellent team. Without subservience on either side, with initiative pretty well distributed between them, they were always in agreement on all matters which touched the welfare of the family. They were meticulous conservationists without being in the slightest degree parsimonious. Each felt free to suggest, to propose, to initiate such humble enterprises as investing the meager savings in a half-dozen hens. They shared a persistent, haunting anxiety about providing for their children the best within their means. That was the secret both of their harmonious relationship and of their ultimate, modest success.

Like all peasants, they worked hard; but unlike all peasants, they brought a certain degree of imagination to their labors. They were not ambitious. They were not "go-getters." They had no grand design in life. They were perfectly willing to remain peasants, to operate within the little world in which they were born. But within that little world they were constantly scheming and plotting to defeat the resistance to their modest desires: adequate food, clean, warm clothing for the children, perhaps a penny or two salted away against emergencies. Nothing more than that. Each day they went about their work, sustained by an active hope that the morrow could be made just a little bit better. Had they lacked these qualities—particularly the sustaining faith, the hope that, with their own efforts, they could eventually provide what they thought their children should have —Father would never have left Italy. And had I survived the Fascist bludgeon, the Ethiopian crusade, the Spanish campaign, and all the madness which followed 1939. . . But these are gross improbabilities. There would have been no sequel to contemplate.

I think it was compassion that finally provoked them to think seriously of America. They had tried their best in Casabianca. They had even ventured so far as France and Algiers. But when they had looked soberly into the future, and taken careful stock of the possibilities available to them, they had seen it only in terms of continued misery, of annoying, marginal existence. Of course we were not starving. There was always an abundance of weeds and vegetables, of beans and corn, of dry cod and stinking pilchards. Furthermore, an Italian never starves! His techniques for survival are miraculous! Those who have had occasion to observe the Neapolitan street urchins, the notorious *scugnitz*, will understand what I mean.

But misery to Father and Mother meant quite something else. I do not mean to imply that they saw—as I can see it now in retrospect—the real tragedy of our existence; nor that they had fancy notions about how the Pellegrinis should live. They were acutely aware of their responsibilities as parents; and they had some idea of the meaning of dignity in human life. For example, there was a certain menace in their reproach when my brother and I were caught in the neighbor's chicken coop sucking eggs like two little demons; but they were also disturbed because they realized that a real necessity had driven their sons to petty robbery, a necessity they had been unable to satisfy. They were anxious that we should wear shoes; and yet when they bought us footwear (not really shoes as we know them in America) they were driven to enjoin its use except in school and in church. So we lugged the wooden sandals under our arm, or strung over the shoulder, until we reached the church or the schoolhouse door. They were outwardly stern when they refused the coin we needed to buy an ice-cream cone, and they tried to put the refusal in terms of some vague discipline; but they knew that they had refused because they did not have the coin. And that hurt them.

They saw our future in terms of repeated frustrations. They perceived, also, what the toll would be on us and on themselves. The kind of gradual starvation which ultimately reduces man, in behavior and in appearance, to the level of the beast, they dreaded most of all. Beyond bread and wine for the stomach, they saw the need of so many little things that children must have to grow in health, in joy, and in decency; and they felt that, if they failed to provide them for their own children, they would live in anxiety and die miserable failures. So to do their duty as they saw it, but more out of a profound compassion for us, they agreed that Father should take a neighbor's advice and go to America.

The neighbor was *l'Americano*, so called because he had been in America and had returned with enough money to realize every peasant's dream: his own home and a bit of land. He told Father fabulous stories about America and urged him to emigrate. "In three years," he said, "you can save enough money to do what I have done. Steerage passage across the Atlantic costs very little. When you arrive in New York the employment agents of the railroad companies will take you to the job at their own expense. If you need money for the steamship ticket I will be glad to lend it to you." And he did.

So Father left for America late in 1912. It was a desperate adventure. He knew no one who would meet him in New York. He had no assurance of a job. He knew nothing of the procedure in looking for one. Crossing the Atlantic was a terrifying prospect to an Italian peasant. It had about it the same smell of doom that the sailors whom Columbus cajoled into accompanying him in 1492 must have experienced. Leaving a wife and five children for three years, or more if luck failed him, must have scarred his heart irreparably.

I have tried without much success to recapture the exact mood of that departure. All I can remember is confusion, tears, a savage kiss; a feeling that separation was final—that Father was going to a far-off place beyond the ocean, and that we should never see him again. And a dim vision of Mother, for weeks thereafter, trying bravely to conceal the tears she could not withhold.

Upon his arrival in New York, Father was immediately employed by the agents of the Northern Pacific Railway and assigned to an "extra gang" which was eventually dispatched to the state of Washington. And it was there that he met Sistrom, who was section foreman for a pioneer firm, the Henry McCleary Timber Co.

Henry McCleary and his two brothers had established the

company at the turn of the century, and by the end of the first decade they were ready to operate on a large scale. They owned extensive timber land, had established a shingle mill and a sawmill, and by the time Father appeared on the scene they were ready to undertake the manufacture of fir doors. They operated their own logging camp and hauled the logs on their own equipment over their own railroad. Father went to work for them and later became Sistrom's assistant. With a gang of about thirty men, all of them Greeks and Italians, the two men constructed and maintained twenty miles of railroad.

Father and Sistrom became close friends. I have frequently wondered about the basis of that friendship. Each spoke a bizarre version of the English language which I could seldom understand. How did they communicate when they first met? They were a strange pair, complete opposites, with apparently nothing in common but their work.

Sistrom was a man of extraordinary strength. His Scandinavian pallor and his unathletic bearing were deceptive. The large, somewhat elliptical head, the heavy neck, and the sloping shoulders formed a single block. His arms hung loosely from his shoulders and paralleled his torso, which was unusually long and tended to a rather deep rotundity. He walked with a lead of the right shoulder and a slight stoop which had nothing to do with age.

He lacked the attributes which ordinarily suggest strength: the square shoulders, the broad chest, the pinched buttocks and narrow waist, the chiseled bulge of the biceps. And he was about as agile and graceful as a bear. He was all of a piece, a roughly molded mass. But he had plenty of primitive, brute power. How much, no one ever knew. Its source was hidden; it just simply met the challenge, whatever it happened to be. I saw him once, observing quietly, as four men struggled to lift a railroad rail with iron tongs. He finally motioned them aside, picked up the rail with his bare hands, and set it neatly in place.

He was quiet and good in a negative rather than a positive way. He minded his own business and was never known to be harsh or cruel. His smile was little else than a slight twitch of the mouth. When he spoke, it was rarely more than a half-dozen words at a time. His diet consisted chiefly of whisky and pancakes, both of which he consumed in huge quantities. But I never saw him drunk, although on occasion he dozed in his chair after having leisurely dispatched the better part of a bottle of rye.

Father was in every way a contrast. He was of medium height, somewhat stocky though well proportioned, and very dark. The high forehead, with the black, curly hair receding beyond the temples, the sparkling, brown, deep-socketed eyes, suggested a man of quality. He had a conservatively elaborate mustache which I believe he cultivated so that he might suck it twice after each glass of wine: a short and a long suck in quick succession. It was a gesture which translated relish into sound.

Although he had no more than the usual three years of elementary education, he was a cultivated peasant with all the instincts of a gentleman. His calligraphy was both legible and distinguished—an attribute which gave him considerable, unsolicited status among his Italian friends. The more so, since he also had a talent for precise, laconic expression, and a knack for untangling issues and keeping the discussion grooved. He did not himself talk excessively. He sat among his friends, listened to their heated arguments, and often dismissed with a nod of the head requests for his opinion. But when he felt inclined to make an observation, and asked for their attention, they listened with respect; for they knew from experience that when Father spoke he usually had something to say.

And he had a taste for good food and good wine. Like so many men who are genuinely interested in food and discriminating in their tastes, he had learned to cook, and he enjoyed cooking whenever he had the opportunity. The cultivated peasant, with the instincts of a gentleman, could be seen regularly at the kitchen range on Sunday: smooth-shaven, black hair parted on the side, the sleeves of the white shirt rolled above the elbows, Mother's embroidered apron tied around his waist, whistling merrily among his pots and pans, in the hot glow of the stove, preparing for his family and his friends the chicken or the rabbit he had dressed the day before.

No man was happier than Father when the food pleased him; and no man more unpleasant when it did not. When the day's work was done he gravitated tremulously toward the dinner table, as if each dinner were the first or the last, or some rare, novel experience. He was not a heavy eater; he ate moderately, but with great care and great relish—almost with deliberation, certainly with absorbed attention. Unlike his friend Sistrom, he seldom drank whisky; but wine was another matter. He approached it as he would approach a friend: with a benediction on his lips. He held the glass of the ruby liquid to the light; he talked to it; he consulted with it; he praised it; he reproached it when its transparence was defective; and he drank it with audible gusto. A quart a day was his measure: a pint in the lunch bucket, a congenial and bracing companion on the job; and a pint at dinner to celebrate the end of another day of honest labor.

Father was excessively cautious in his total behavior, something of a perfectionist in all his undertakings. So much so that, in consequence, he undertook little. Only in his work, in the home and on the job, was he reckless and unsparing of himself. In all else he was somewhat like Hamlet: too much given to weighing consequences. He was particularly diffident in making generalizations. However, when Prohibition came upon him like a curse, he threw caution to the winds and quickly branded the noble experiment as the Unforgivable Heresy.

Such were Father and Sistrom. Superficially they were poles apart; but there was something below the surface in each which brought them together in a genuine friendship. I was never quite certain that I knew what it was. When they talked about their common work they understood each other fairly well; but when they talked of other matters—Or did they ever talk about other matters? I did not know; for when Sistrom came into our home —which he did frequently—and sat with us at dinner he did little else than twitch his face into a smile and pinch gently the cheeks of my little sisters. I was curious about that friendship because I attributed to it the most important event in my life: a thirty days' journey into a New World and to good fortune.

—*Immigrant's Return*

LA BIMBINA

ANYONE WHO PASSED by her house on October 15, 1948, at about five in the afternoon, might have seen her at work in the garden: a small, stoutish woman, a little bent with age, gray hair gathered neatly in a knot at the back of the head, dressed in a plain cotton garment faded by many washings. At about that time she had finished setting out a bed of garlic for her family that extended to three generations scattered in various parts of the Northwest. It was one of the little ways in which she continued to look after the needs of her children, who had long since left the immigrant homestead to which she had taken them on the eve of World War I; and some of whom had become so well adjusted to American urban life as to exclude the possibility of growing their own aromatics.

She smiled as she surveyed the straight rows and the rich black earth that she had tilled for so many years; for she knew that the children would come, as they had come in years past, and that each would return to his own home, bearing with him the garlic, the flowers, the herbs, and whatever other produce from Mother's garden happened to suit his fancy. And she knew, too, that they would come frequently and unannounced because there was a bond between them and herself and the little plot of earth that had been their first home in America. Her smile reflected all this—and a mother's life marred by no major regrets.

She gathered the tools and brought them to the shed, then returned to the garden with her harvest basket. Singing softly an old Italian song,

Guarda che bella luna,
Che brilla in mezzo al mare,
Vieni con me a vogare,
Insieme co' i marinar....

she gathered bits of celery, parsley, chard, savoy cabbage, zucchini, a few fresh roman beans, and brought them to the kitchen, there to be converted into a savory vegetable soup for the evening meal.

She made the *soffritto* of herbs and salt pork, added a large, ripe tomato, and left the ingredients to simmer while she washed and cut the vegetables. These she put into the pot and stirred thoroughly in the aromatic sauce. When the vegetables were partially cooked she added salt, pepper, and a bit of boiling water, set the pot to one side on the spacious surface of the wood range, and went to her bedroom to dress for lodge meeting.

She had a peasant's love for early autumn—an unsophisticated love for September and October which had little to do with the aesthetic qualities poets have discovered in these months. She was no doubt aware of the low-hanging harvest moon, of the gradual change in the color of the landscape, and of the increasing chill in the twilight air. She saw, too, in her own garden, that the rose and the violet had given way to the salvia and the zinnia. And she was wise enough to see in the yellow leaf a reminder of her own mortality. I am sure she was pleasantly aware of these suggestive attributes of the fall months; but the source of her sustained delight in them lay in her antecedents as an immigrant mother of peasant stock.

It was during this season that she had known for many years the twofold joy of planting and reaping. For over half a century she had gathered the yield of the spring sowing and stocked the cellar shelves against the bleak winter months. Then into the soil, still warm with the lingering sun, she had placed the seed of the turnip, the pea, the broad bean, and the garlic—all to be reaped the following spring. And for the late fall and early winter she had set out in the Septembers past the tiny plants of endive, kale, black cabbage, leeks, and second plantings of celery, chard, and savoy cabbage, the hardy vegetables which she found so indispensable in her excellent cuisine.

And as the years had passed, the early autumn had come to have a further, more intimate meaning to her. When the homestead had been established by her husband years ago, he had planted a winesap apple, a Bartlett pear, and two Italian plum trees. Those trees had grown to full stature and were yielding abundant crops. She remembered with what diligence her good man, now long since dead, had cared for them, and how proud he had been of the first fruit they had borne. In a different context, the trees had become for her as the sheepfold to old Michael after the disaffection of his son. There were other legacies he had left behind; but she had rooted her affection on the fruit trees because they were living symbols of his devotion to the family. It had seemed to her that through them he continued his contributions to the family's keep. So she had come to anticipate with a certain quiet joy the successive seasons when she could harvest the fruit and distribute it in equal portions to the children. It had become a kind of unconscious symbol in which they participated gladly, frequently driving several hundred miles to the homestead at harvesttime.

"Mother, let me know when the fruit is ripe" had been a request she had come to expect from them as each summer had drawn to a close.

And then, too, she loved the early autumn because the garden produce then made possible the best variant of her vegetable soup. The savoy cabbage, the shelled roman beans, and the tip ends of the zucchini vines she considered the ingredients par excellence in the vegetable soup which she ate almost daily for dinner. And on that evening she ate it with unusual relish—a large bowl with toasted and buttered homemade bread lightly rubbed with garlic—because a hard day in the garden had given edge to her appetite; but more so because it was simple fare made with her own fresh produce, in the salutary quality of which she had an almost mystical faith. *Nella vecchiaia bisogna accostare la tavola con prudenza.* (In old age one must approach the dinner table with prudence.)

When she had washed the dishes and cleaned the kitchen, she set out to walk the short distance to the hall of the Knights of Pythias. On the way she met her old neighbor, Pietro Fornili, leading his Jersey cow home from the pasture.

"*Ei, Bimbina, andate forse alla messa vestita così bene?*" (Well, well, Bimbina, I suppose you are all dolled up to go to church?)

"*Via, via, Pietro, non prendetemi in giro. Tutti lo sanno che in paese mi aspetta il fidanzato.*" (Come, come, Pietro, don't kid me. Everyone knows that my beau is waiting for me in the village.)

At ten past nine that evening, when the meeting of her lodge was about to be adjourned, she died quickly and unexpectedly in the arms of one of the sisters.

Death came to her appropriately at the end of the day's labor. She had lived seventy-four years, on three continents, and had borne six children whom she had seen married and established, each in his own home. She had shared with them the first frightening anxieties of parenthood and had minimized their terror with her easy talent for subduing adversity. Because she had given birth to her own brood with only the crudest obstetrical aid, and had nursed them all successfully, she had acquired a reassuring confidence in the many crises infant flesh is heir to. Whooping cough, the mumps, the measles, scarlatina—all of these she had dismissed, with laughter and words of encouragement, as mere trifles. "*Niente; assolutamente niente! Vedrai che domani saltellerà come un capretto.*" (Nothing! It's nothing at all! Tomorrow he will hop and skip like a billy goat. You shall see!)

As the children had radiated in various directions from the homestead, she had become a sort of peripatetic nurse. Always ready, always indefatigable, always cheerful, she had gone from the home of one to that of another, assisting the mothers through postnatal convalescence and teaching them the little tricks of infant care. There had been sixteen grandchildren and great-grandchildren who had called her *Nonna* and to whom she had taught the gay little songs, French and Italian, that had delighted her own little ones.

After the death of her husband she had added his burdens to her own and completed the task they had begun together in Italy at the close of the last century. She had increased the little substance he had left, and improved the immigrant homestead. A mother's impartial love of her children was reflected in the will she had prepared; and among her personal effects she had tucked away a receipt for a grave adjoining that of her husband.

She died appropriately, as if by design, at the end of the day's labor. The fall planting had been done. The fruit had been harvested and distributed to the children. The plum jam had been prepared for three generations of offspring. Unto the very last she had worked with her hands that those to whom she had given life might have their daily quota of bread and wine, and that she, as a good Christian, might justify her existence.

Worked with her hands! They were small hands, but thick, with bulging knuckles and cracked skin—hands that had never known the dubious luxury of idle hours. They had woven and spun and carded flax; they had tilled the soil, wielded sickle and scythe, and held the spade and the hoe in their firm grip. They had cut the grape, pruned the vine, and stripped leaves from the mulberry tree to feed the silkworm. They had washed clothes, made tons of bread, scrubbed floors, and prepared innumerable meals. They had come finally to rest, folded one inside the other, in the traditional posture of death. *Noialtri che non abbiamo educazione bisogna avere giudizio nelle mani.* (We who have no education must have good sense in our hands.)

She was one among millions who at the turn of the century fled the denuded corners of the earth, fled penury and indignity, want of the flesh and want of the soul driven by despair and enticed by a new hope. They came positively and determined to our prodigal shores, where they knew there was work to do and the means to realize every peasant's dream: a permanent home. Some found more than they had dared to hope for; la Bimbina found labor. And through labor, a measure of fulfillment.

The trip from her native village in Tuscany to a frontier village in western Washington where she went to join her husband was not an easy one. There were five children in tow —the sixth was born here—ranging in age from three to fifteen years. The passage across the Atlantic was rough, frightening, and exhausting. After nineteen days of uncertain tossing, crowded in the filthy steerage of an ancient ship, where the smell of vomit mingled with the odor of boiling cod in the galley, they reached Ellis Island. Then followed the bewildering journey across the continent, across plains, mountains, and rivers—six long days, always among strangers with whom communication was impossible, and the children, restless and hungry, asking questions no one could answer, and never once the restorative balm of untroubled sleep.

The little home that her husband had prepared, the village in which it was situated, and the surrounding country were not, at first glance, the immigrant's dream of America. The town had a primitive and inhuman quality, even an appearance of instability, as if it had been hurriedly put together by some wandering tribe for temporary shelter. It appeared at once very old and very young.

Indeed, the entire setting had a quality of virginal prim-
itivism to which her Italian eyes were unaccustomed. The forest at the back door, the ugly frame shacks, the grass-covered
streets and unstable board walks were such a sharp contrast to the
humanized Italian landscape that they gave an initial impression
of poverty rather than of wealth.

But la Bimbina was quick to appraise the possibilities and
to accept the challenge. The new environment was an invitation
to work. There were board walks in disrepair, grass at the
doorsteps, dwellings of wood hastily and carelessly put together
because there was so much of everything that the natives had
acquired neither the habit of work nor the idea of permanence
in what they did. Because these were central attributes in her
character, she accepted her new home with gratitude.

She rolled up her sleeves and fell to the task. Within a year
her contributions to the family income were somewhat in excess
of her husband's wages. There were cows, pigs, chickens, and
rabbits in a barn that had been built with waste lumber from the
mill. Land abutting the family property, never before touched by
human hands, was soon producing for the table and for the
animals. Surplus milk, eggs, and poultry were sold to the vil-
lagers. Occasionally there were pork and beef to be exchanged
for other necessities at the local store. Of the immigrant bachelors
who had begged to share her cheerful home, some were taken
in, and they paid well for their board; others had to be satisfied
with sharing the Sunday dinner and having their laundry done.

These resources she tapped on her own initiative; for her
man worked ten strenuous hours daily, in fair weather and foul,

at the lumber camp. Except for the occasional aid that he could give, the main burden fell upon herself and the children. And la Bimbina knew how to harness their energy shrewdly and sternly. "*Venite subito a casa dopo la scuola o vi sbuccio come si fa a un ranocchio!*" (Come immediately home after school or I'll skin you as I would a frog!) Such imperatives, delivered with a clenched fist and a penetrating eye, were completely effective with children who had observed a thousand times the skill with which she "undressed" a sackful of croakers.

And so the two boys practiced their right and their left jabs at the kneading trough twice weekly and learned early in life to make an excellent bread—a salutary lesson. They worked in the garden, gathered wood, tended the animals, sold and delivered the surplus produce. The girls labored at the endless tasks in the home and did more than, in retrospect, it was fair to ask of them. But there was work to be done, the handicap of many lean years to overcome. And in the excitement of the abundant present and the peasant's perpetual anxiety about the future, la Bimbina drove her young ones with a relentless urgency that she later regretted.

But in fairness to the children, and to their credit, it must be acknowledged that they all worked with more willingness and sustained enthusiasm than is common among youngsters. For each was old enough to remember the futility of toil in a land of scarcity, and to be excited by the immediate and tangible rewards of labor in their new home. They found an enduring fascination in the wooded hills where berries, nuts, and game awaited their eager hands. There were abandoned orchards in which they could pick apples, plums, and pears by the sack.

There were meadows of clover which was a joy to cut for the rabbits. There were refuse heaps where they could salvage liquor bottles for sale to the druggist at a penny apiece.

They responded feverishly to the abundance around them and they worked like little heroes. But still, they were children: and had their mother been less exemplary in the behavior she expected of them, less shrewd in her grasp of what the new home offered, and less exacting in the demands of what she knew they could give, they would have succumbed soon enough to the more indolent mood of their strange new associates.

Her Italian friends, with an uncanny talent for summarizing a character in a single word, called her *Bimbina*, which is a slight Tuscan perversion of *bambina*—little girl. The name described perfectly her infectious gaiety, her love of life, her utter ingenuousness in dealing with people of superior rank, and her willingness to participate in any community mood that brought hearts closer together. That is why she was always included in the gatherings of the young. They seemed to sense that she could express with the authority of age the abandon they felt but about the propriety of which they were, on occasion, a little uncertain.

She had the gift of laughter and a rare sensibility of the heart which delighted old friends and disarmed strangers. The *paesani* called on her frequently, especially after the death of her husband. Some of them traveled a long distance to be with la Bimbina. They took her on jaunts to the seaside, to mountain resorts, or to the city. They urged her to go with them on their vacations that they, who had known her intimately in the village of their birth, might laugh together and recall days past in the Florentine countryside. And they found her always ready to go, smiling as she untied her kitchen apron.

I saw her last at the engagement party of one of her grand-sons, just a few months before her death. It was a typical Italian affair, held at the rather swanky home of the young lady's parents. The guests, as is common among Italians, had come in family units; so that life in its various stages was represented in the spacious recreation room. Men, women, and children were seated along the four walls on bright, chrome steel chairs with upholstered seats, as if they awaited instructions from a master of ceremonies.

The disparity in wealth between the host and his guests made the latter a little more diffident than is usual on such occasions. They were somewhat awed by the display: the large room with its floor of shining oak, the expensive fixtures, the movie camera manned by an expert operator, the table weighted with more food than twice the number of guests could consume, the bar presided over by two bartenders in uniform, the orches-tra. They sat in a kind of collective uncertainty and smiled politely as the accordion, guitar, and mandolin wheezed and twanged their invitation to song and dance and laughter.

Those who knew la Bimbina were secretly calculating how long it would be before she kicked up her heels and got things going, for they knew that in such a gathering she was the allegro movement in a major key. They did not wait very long. When she had had enough of the funereal atmosphere, she walked across the floor to the musicians and after a brief consultation burst into song. In a high strained voice in which the overflowing heart completely dominated technique, she sang the song that was in the hearts of the two lovers:

Vieni dolce amore ti voglio baciare
Se mi sai baciare ti do tutto il cuore....

The heart valves were opened wide. Old and young alike followed her in song and then in a spirited waltz which she led with one of her sons. *Il Penseroso* disappeared from the room and *l'Allegro* ruled the roost until three o'clock in the morning.

Her gaiety never wholly surrendered to grief and pain of which she certainly had more than her share; and although a happy heart was nature's gift to her, in America her joy deepened its roots and found nourishment on a new substance: the absolute assurance, overwhelming as well in its novelty as in its reality, *that here there was work to do.*

Here there was work to do! To find work that would satisfy her family's need had been her quest; the work was found, and it became the dominating reality in her life. She radiated joy. She inspired laughter. Meeting her was a tonic. Knowing her intimately was a memorable experience. And the frontier village, to which she had come as an outcast and in which she caught a glimpse of the meaning of human dignity, will long remember her influence.

She could be best described as an intelligent isolationist. Her busy life in Italy, in France, in Algiers, and finally in America had taught her that every individual must function within two orbits: in the home and in the community. She knew the frequently subtle difference between one's own and everybody's affairs; and although she may on occasion have confused the two she never stepped beyond her garden gate until she felt that a larger interest summoned her to action. A reputation for tending to her own affairs, and the honor of having been chosen one of two women who had done most for the community, are testimony to the accuracy of her judgment on such matters.

Anyone within her sphere who was guilty of a palpable injustice knew that sooner or later he would have to reckon with la Bimbina. It mattered little who were the offender and the victim; and she was inclined to be most severe with those who were closest to her. Her tactics on such occasions were conciliatory, disarming, and persistent. She smiled and asked embarrassing questions. The chronic tippler who neglected his work and endangered the security of his family, and with whom no one could cope, she would search out in the pool hall and bring home to his family. "Do you want to lose your job? Don't you know that your children need your help? Aren't you ashamed, with your wife home crying? Now come home and behave like a man; and when you want a drink come to my house."

The tippler lied that he had just been home. He promised that he would have another drink and then go immediately. But she smiled and stayed with him until he followed her out, unable to resist the appeal of her generous spirit; and also because he had learned from experience that to refuse meant only that he would have to confront her later, weakened by his hangover.

The executives of the timber mill and camp, in their independence typical of the rugged exploiters of the West, found in her an adversary who was not easily awed by power. They employed almost exclusively immigrant labor, Greeks and Italians to whom la Bimbina had become a mother. It was in the days before unionization, and the millowners wielded absolute power.

When la Bimbina learned that one of them had been dismissed she made a single inquiry: Did the man have a reputation for being a hard worker? If so, she confronted the "big boss." She smiled shrewdly, the smile of one who knows he is on the side of the angels; and by the sheer force of her ingenuous attack, delivered in a bizarre jargon compounded of Italian, French, and English, she compelled reinstatement.

There may have been technical reasons and, as such, adequate enough for the dismissal. But the secret of her power lay in a mind unencumbered by a perception of even the most elementary legalisms. Her heart and not her mind was the seat of justice. She could penetrate very quickly to the irreducible reality and produce the unanswerable argument. "There is work to do. The man is a good worker. He has a wife and children who need bread. Well?"

Wherever she intervened, no matter what the issue involved, one felt immediately a benign presence whose appeal could not be easily resisted. For want of words she had to be brief; and in being brief she cut through to the reality that in others is frequently lost in excessive verbiage. "The children need bread. Well?" That is an embarrassing question when asked by one who cannot be engaged in verbal distractions. And, more frequently than not, it is, in its context, the humane question.

And thus she made everyone feel the importance of the heart in human relations. By remaining suggestively close to life, she reminded her contemporaries that we are born to live and that we must learn to live together, and that any activity, any preoccupation that is not inspired by this basic truth leads inevitably to personal grief and to collective wretchedness.

When her husband died, as the result of an industrial accident, her claim to a pension from the state required proof that death was caused by the injury. The physicians, with their characteristic ambivalence in such cases, failed in their report to satisfy the state that the claim came within the provisions of the statute. The lawyers whom she had procured to present her case returned convinced that nothing could be done. She went to the state capitol herself. Armed with a single argument, and with an angel sitting on either shoulder, she smiled and entered the office of the commissioner of industrial insurance for the State of Washington.

"My husband worked at the mill for ten years. He was never sick. One day his chest was crushed between two railroad cars. He never returned to work. In six months he was dead. Who is to feed me and the children? Well?"

The good man had listened to many petitions. In protecting the interests of the state he had opposed many lawyers; but he had never had to cope with an argument so short, so novel, so irrefutable. In his arsenal of regulations, there was nothing adequate to the purpose. He reversed his decision; and he became la Bimbina's friend and adviser. Well?

She left the office happy and a little proud. In her purse was a check for all that was due her from the state to date. When she arrived home she thrust the check under the nose of one of her lawyers. "*Se avessi la vostra educazione!*" (If I only had your education!)

Se avessi la vostra educazione! This conditional threat was her constant reproach to whoever had had the benefit of years in school, and yet failed in any important undertaking. It was hurled most frequently at her children, through clenched teeth and with brandished fist. There were defiance, disgust, impatience, and a deep yearning of the heart in that exclamation. It was a compressed biography and a commentary on a whole society.

At sixty-five, when the children were married and she had at last achieved some leisure, she went to school for the first time. In a new print dress, her wavy white hair neatly and severely brushed, she went up the path, along which she had accompanied her children twenty-five years before, to the square frame structure on top of the hill. A little self-conscious, she stepped across the threshold and took her seat.

la Bimbina would learn to read and write. She would study the Declaration of Independence and the Constitution. And then she would ask to be admitted to citizenship in the United States of America. At sixty-five years of age! *"Strano paese, l'America!"* (Strange land, America!)

The experience was novel and the challenge formidable; but she accepted both with characteristic enthusiasm. She made the teacher, Flora E. Arland, her intimate friend, and took immense delight in everything she learned. She brought laughter to the classroom; and for the occasional party she sang, she made the coffee, and baked the bread.

When she walked out of the Superior Court of Grays Harbor County, in March, 1940, a citizen of the United States, she was a proud little lady. Mrs. Arland had prepared her for the examination with affectionate care; la Bimbina had enjoyed the kindly probing questions put to her by the judge. But there had been one rather panicky moment.

She was asked to recite the preamble to the Constitution. Grasping firmly the arms of the chair and bending slightly forward, she began: " 'We, the people of the United States, in order to form a more perfect Union, establish justice, insure domestic tranquillity, provide for the common defense, promote the general *hwarfare* ...' "

"Promote what?" interjected the judge.

"Well, 'the general *hwar-fare, hwar-fare,*' " she replied, repeating the word more slowly the second time.

"Do you mean wel-fare?" asked the judge.

"Yes, that's I say: *hwar-fare, hwarfare.*" And so it had to remain; for in her very special version of the English language it could not be otherwise.

Yes, she was a proud little lady; but not for the usual reasons. Of course, she was happy to be a citizen, and she was anticipating the pleasure of casting her first ballot; but beyond that her enthusiasm did not extend, for she had no illusions about politics. She had lived under five Presidents, two Democrats and three Republicans; and, as she often observed, "*Ho lavorato duro per tutti.*" (I have worked hard for all of them.)

la Bimbina was proud because the discipline to which she had submitted was her first skirmish with books—and she had won! The achievement was modest and it had come late. She could turn it to no practical use. But it was a victory whence she derived much satisfaction; for while she brought an exuberant confidence and shrewd resourcefulness to the world of labor, she had been dubious about her aptitude in the world of learning. And, of course, notwithstanding that she was frequently disappointed in men who had enjoyed its benefits, she had a deep respect for education. So the discovery that she, too—she, the hardy peasant whose strong, thick hands had never held a book —was capable of formal learning had made her very happy.

Se avessi la vostra educazione! What she really meant was that if she could only read, write, and speak the English language she would feel equal to any task. Immigrants generally, after repeated failures to express themselves in words, come to have some such understandably naive faith in the magic of language. But there was more than that in la Bimbina's attitude. She was too wise to be impressed by idle words. *Chiacchiere, chiacchiere, e non si fa niente* (Chatter, chatter, and we accomplish nothing) had been her frequent, caustic observation in council, whether at home or at community meetings. Or she would whip out the appropriate proverb: *Ragazzi, questa vigna non fa uva.* (Boys, this vineyard produces no grapes.)

Her high regard for the ability to read, write, and speak the English language was rooted in quite something else. She was an individual uniquely and extraordinarily proud. Of family? Personal accomplishments? Nationality? She was never known to boast about such trifles. She was proud of being a human being, alive and full of daring, in a world where there was so much to be done, where there were so many petty fellow creatures to chastise, and of herself feeling able to do so much and feeling it with a haunting urgency.

"You are too easily beaten by injustice and adversity. You lack gall, spirit, initiative." *In questo mondo ci vuol coraggio!*

In this, her most frequent criticism of her fellows, she revealed an important side of her own nature. She had a driving will and an abundance of spiritual energy; but she lacked the means for giving them the direction she saw so clearly. As the years passed she became increasingly aware of what she might have accomplished had not the circumstances of birth and the vicissitudes of a hard life deprived her of the means necessary to cultivate her talents. It was the one frustration in an otherwise remarkably integrated life.

Especially in America, where she spent the last half of her life, where she found so much to appreciate, so much to criticize, and so much to do, she felt constantly the urgings of a generous heart and the spur of a keen mind. But always there was the annoying barrier of a bewildering language, and no time to master it beyond the degree necessary to satisfy her simplest requirements. It is little wonder that she came to equate education with the ability to read, write, and speak the English language.

And yet, despite this limitation, which in serious crises she simply refused to recognize, her influence on the community was appreciable. It was not an influence easily defined. Especially during the last decade she participated widely in community affairs but was never in nominal leadership. She was not an organizer and she was inclined to be a little suspicious of organizations as such. In the groups to which she belonged she did the little things she could do best: she sang, she cooked, she collected funds—with amazing success—and she made things with her hands.

But the source of her influence on the village lay elsewhere; and to understand it we must look a little more closely at la Bimbina as a mother and homemaker. It was her total behavior in the community that inspired her neighbors to search within themselves and to reexamine their way of life.

She was a mother first of all; and in being a good mother, harassed on occasion to the point where she would exclaim, "A nest of scorpions would be a greater blessing than you brats," she could not avoid being a good citizen. Her children were always clean, always well fed, always in leash, always compelled to assume the burdens appropriate to their years. She was suspicious of surface frills and finery as camouflage for dirt behind the ears; and as she scrubbed her lusty brood and examined their undergarments she reminded them that one never knew when one might be kicked by a mule and find it necessary to be undressed by a stranger. Impressed by this frightening and somewhat anachronistic possibility, the young ones submitted to soap and tub and learned a valuable lesson.

The neatness, cleanliness, and bucolic simplicity of her home and her person reflected an experienced husbandry that in America is a neglected virtue. The garden was well kept and productive, a constant reminder that she had come to America not to exploit but to labor and to enjoy and conserve the earth and its fruit. Her cellar was always stocked as if the danger of being snowbound were ever present.

It was this sense of economy that was the best clue to her wisdom, expressed in a series of bedrock absolutes from which she never deviated: it is wrong to waste. It is wrong to depend on others when one has strength. It is wrong not to provide for an uncertain future. It is wrong not to be able to offer bread and wine to the unexpected guest. It is wrong to refuse aid to those in need. This solicitude for her family and for all others who came within her orbit integrated into a larger significance her industry and frugality. It gave to these simple virtues a meaning that in a less humane spirit they do not possess.

In obedience to this unsophisticated credo she worked and conserved. Every fall she converted the yield of two plum trees into jam for her friends and three generations of her offspring. In accord with a tradition, sacred among Italians, that the cellar should be stocked with choice wines against periods of illness and convalescence, her children and friends had kept her well supplied over a period of years. *"Bimbina, alla vostra età ci vuole vino buono."* (Bimbina, at your age you need good wine.) Apparently she had not heeded their advice; for what they had not consumed themselves during their frequent visits was found at her death in the protective custody of cobwebs. And in the trunks that had crossed the Atlantic was stored sturdy linen she had woven with her hands nearly half a century before her death.

It was in these unpretentious ways that she exerted her influence on the community; and the status of the men who carried her body to the grave reflected perfectly, as if by design, the extent to which she had penetrated the life of the village. There were Joe Tincani and Guido Ciloni, two immigrant laborers whom she had taken into her home and to whom she had been a mother for three decades. There were Duke Sherwood, Pete Townsend, and Ernest Teagle, three executives in the Henry McCleary Timber Company. And there was Len McCleary himself, the last survivor of the McCleary brothers who founded the town that bears their name.

As I saw those six men standing at the graveside, in final tribute to an Italian peasant who had come to America in search of bread for her children, I became suddenly aware of a symbolic meaning that, for the moment, eased my own personal grief. They were the representatives of two cultures, those six men, and of both sides of the tracks. The symbol was wholly fortuitous; and as I reflected upon its meaning in terms of America's future I remembered lines by the great Walt Whitman whom time may yet prove, we fervently hope, to have been our most accurate prophet. *Here is not merely a nation but a teeming nation of nations.* America!

Centre of equal daughters, equal sons,
All, all alike endear'd, grown, ungrown, young or old,
Strong, ample, fair, enduring, capable, rich,
Perennial with the Earth, with Freedom, Law and Love,
A grand, sane, towering, seated Mother,
Chair'd in the adamant of Time.

In recalling these lines I heard in them the voices of my best teachers and of all authentic Americans I have known; and for a brief while I forgot that the body of my Mother was being lowered into the grave.

—*Americans by Choice*

OLD GRAND DAD

WHEN MY FATHER worked as a section hand for the Henry McCleary Timber Company in 1913, his foreman was a Swedish immigrant by the name of Swan Sistrom. While he was recruiting men to work for Henry McCleary, he had met my father in a saloon somewhere in the state of Washington, where he was then working as a section hand for the Northern Pacific, and persuaded him to accept similar employment in McCleary.

That chance encounter had in it from the very beginning the elements of a flawless friendship. The bond between them was what the monks of the early church meant when they said *Laborare est orare*: Labor is a form of worship. Each perceived in the other the dignity and integrity of their craft, the construction and maintenance of railroads, at a time when all such labor was done without mechanical aid.

Within a year Sistrom had made Father his assistant foreman; then he advised him to send for his wife and five children. Thereafter, Sistrom was a frequent visitor in our home, usually on Sundays. The two sat at the kitchen table after the midday dinner, a study in contrast, reciprocal admiration, and perfect communication. Sistrom was a man of great strength. His Scandinavian pallor and unathletic bearing were deceptive. He walked with the lead of the right shoulder and a slight stoop which had nothing to do with age. A quiet fellow, a bit shy, and never mean, Sistrom ate and drank quantities of whiskey from a bottle he always brought with him when he came to our home; Father dined and sipped wine.

A virtue of that flawless friendship was the total adequacy of their communication. And this was the more remarkable for the fact that Sistrom's version of the English language was difficult to understand, while Father knew only a few words of it.

A certain Sunday afternoon that I remember most vividly, when Sistrom and Father sat at the kitchen table, the one drinking whiskey from a bottle that he kept on the floor by his chair, and the other drinking heartily of wine poured from a gallon jug on the table, occurred during a time when the two were planning and constructing a strategic spur from the main track in the valley to a logging site on a hill. It was a considerable feat, for when completed it was thought to be the steepest railroad grade in the logging country. So the two civil engineers in command of thirty men, all Greeks and Italians skilled with the pick and shovel, merry and willing workers in the New Land, had much to talk about in the lingo of their craft.

I was there, full of admiration for my father and his Scandinavian buddy. Then a lad of sixteen, a serious student, now as fluent in English as in Italian, having just completed the eighth grade, I had a sort of academic interest in that rare companionship. And what I am about to record might not have happened had I not been there. For when Father had had his measure of wine, he became strangely interested in the whiskey. Strangely, I say, for he had never shown any interest in the bottle that Sistrom always brought with him. Since Father believed that when he had drunk his measure of wine he could see things a little more clearly and a little more happily, had he exceeded his measure on that occasion?

My father reached for the bottle, looked at it intently, then asked me, "What is this *veesky*?" It was Old Grand Dad, which translated as Vecchio Nonno. Father repeated the name, looked again at the bottle, and remembered that his father, whom we all called Nonno, the Italian for granddad, had been fond of a brandy called Vecchio Romano. Then he made a fatal inference. "Nonno was bitten by a viper at age eighty-eight and survived by drinking a glass of Vecchio Romano," he said. Whereupon the man who was habitually cautious and judicious reasoned, transcendentally no less, that the therapeutic virtue of Vecchio Romano must be also in Vecchio Nonno. Forgetting that he had not been bitten by a viper, he drank half a glass of Old Grand Dad.

Soon thereafter he left abruptly and stumbled his way to the privy in the barn about fifty yards away. Sistrom, sensing what had happened, smiled and took another swig. Having waited a reasonable time, I went to the barn and into the privy. Father was mired in his partially digested Sunday dinner. There were the reddish telltale traces: roast chicken, spaghetti, bread, green beans. Sheepish, bleary-eyed, unsteady on his feet, Father clung to me as I led him into the house. I helped him to remove his clothing and put him to bed, gave him water and put a wet towel on his forehead. "*Il Vecchio Nonno mi ha tradito*," he said. Old Grand Dad has betrayed me.

Sistrom waited until I returned to assure him that Father was all right and sound asleep. Then he drank what was left of the whiskey, grinned knowingly, and with a slight stoop and lead of the right shoulder, he walked away with that rectitude that is the norm of whiskey-drinking Scandinavian gentlemen.

The next day, on the job, the two men must have discussed the betrayal in their inimitable jargon, for Father said he had been unable to convince Sistrom that Vecchio Nonno was traitorous. He had merely grunted at the allegation. But Father knew better and he never gave it another chance. That evening he dined, had his measure of wine, and saw things a little more clearly and a little more happily, which is the norm among wine-sipping Italian gentlemen.

Sistrom was a benedict, and so fond of us children that he always brought us chewing gum and candy bars. Father persuaded him to marry his housekeeper so that he might have children of his own. The wedding was duly celebrated, Italian-style. And that put an end to their Sunday afternoon drinking bouts. But Father kept a bottle of Old Grand Dad on hand. It was still in the pantry, the seal unbroken, when I went to college years later, a reminder that Father's will was indomitable. It was opened after Father's death when we celebrated my youngest sister's wedding. Since I was the firstborn son and now head of the family, I presided over the festivities. And what the traitorous Vecchio Nonno did to me on that occasion is a deep dark secret.

—*Seattle Weekly*

My Father's
Suspenders

PIACENTO PELLEGRINI, MY father, was swarthy, of medium height and thick in the chest. When he was in a good mood the expression on his face inspired confidence and affection; but when he was angry or just simply in a bad mood he was stern, touchy, uncongenial.

One Sunday morning after church, in Casabianca in Tuscan Italy, he called his children into the kitchen. One glance at his face and we knew it was not a friendly summons.

"Where is it? Who has it? Answer me!" Bang, bang, bang, his words like pistol shots! "Stand here, all of you! Where is the script?"

He meant a handwritten script to a folk drama, *Il testamento*, in which he annually played a small role. Our only answer was a shrug of the shoulders.

He stood before us, the image of power and authority, menace written in his black, piercing eyes. "One of you is guilty, and if you don't confess within two minutes..."

He looked at his watch. Trembling with chilling fear, we

looked at each other for consolation as he began slowly to un-buckle his heavy leather belt. We had been threatened with it before, but had never known its sting. This time, however, there seemed to be no way of avoiding it. We had been expecting the usual treat after church—thin pancakes made with chestnut flour overspread with ricotta—not an undeserved punishment.

We were two girls and two boys ranging in age between twelve and five. I was seven and his firstborn son. My brother was five. Father looked particularly at me, for according to pri-mogeniture I would succeed as master of the household, a grave responsibility that required the strictest honesty.

In the sepulchral stillness of that holy morning, his slow, deliberate threat roared in our ears. Mother, in her fifth preg-nancy, was standing behind us. Was she convinced of our inno-cence? Would she prevent an injustice?

In conducting the affairs of the family, our parents planned and executed jointly; but in the matters of discipline there was a sort of division of labor. Mother presided over misdemeanors, Father, over felonies. That was the law, and it was clearly un-derstood, as was also our code of behavior as children of caring and reasonable parents. So we knew, or were told if we did not, whether for a given infraction we would receive a spanking and a fierce scolding from Mother, or a beating from Father.

Thus far we had several of the former but none of the lat-ter. Mother's indulgence and the ever-present threat had given Father no occasion to unbuckle his belt. A bold lie, thievery no matter how petty, any abuse of Mother, were some of the felonies for which there was no forgiveness. What there was of conscience in children loved and of normally good behavior had been enough to resist any temptation to lie or steal or be unkind to Mother, but not necessarily to keep the hand out of the cookie jar. Since we were peasants there was, of course, no cookie jar; but you get what I mean.

And now we were accused of a felony I knew *I* did not commit. I had no reason to believe one of the others was guilty, for each had repeatedly asserted his innocence. If, however, one was, the rest of us hoped that he or she would confess. If there are cases in which circumstantial evidence is to be as conclusive as direct evidence, ours was certainly their prototype. And Father was certain that it was all against us.

We children had been trained by Mother to respect Father's dark moods by silence at the table and exemplary behavior. Whether he was in a good mood or bad depended on the family's larder. Was there enough bread for the day? Would there be enough tomorrow? Had he had good luck in hunting snipes, or catching frogs in the swamp near our home? Had he been fairly paid for work he occasionally did for a rich landowner? Being a father whose principal concern was providing for his family, such little things were the big things in his life. When he seemed preoccupied and Mother saw mischief brewing, she unobtrusively shot a glance at us and put her index finger to her lips, meaning, "*Il babbo è in pensiero*"—Dad is thinking. Doing this in such a way that Father would not be aware of it required tact.

We cultivated a few acres of land as sharecroppers. Corn, wheat, and beans were the main crops. There were chickens and rabbits. We raised a pig. We also raised silkworms, feeding them leaves of the mulberry tree, and when they had transformed themselves into cocoons, we brought them to market at a time that coincided with the cherry harvest. And tradition required that children should be generously rewarded with that delicacy.

We all worked on those acres. Children began when they were about kindergarten age, and there was much they could do. Both family and animals were fed by what was grown on that bit of land. Their waste and ours was used as fertilizer. The privy, a sunken tank in a corner of the barn, had an opening about a foot in diameter, with a tight-fitting lid. To use it, one removed the lid and simply squatted over the hole. It was not a posture that invited loitering. The sewage was later taken up with a bucket affixed to a pole, mixed with water, and carried to the field. Thus we returned to the land the recycled waste of its produce that fed us. Primitive? Without knowing it, we were living in harmony with Nature.

It was somewhat more than a marginal existence. Had we owned the land, our life would have been graced with some of the fattiness that raises it above the level of bare necessities. But there were compensations: we were a healthy, happy family of willing workers; Mother was resourceful in managing the home; Father had mastered the art of managing the land. He was now teaching me how to properly turn the sod with the spade, how to use the rake and the hoe, how to pull weeds without disturbing the plants they infested. And he was now calling me, his firstborn son and successor, *mio uomo*—my man. The effect of that, intended or not, tended to make me strive toward manly behavior.

The work, though continuous, was not heavy. Such seasonal tasks as cornhusking and flailing wheat were done with the aid of neighbors, enlivened by friendly competition and followed by a celebration. The work was done on the hard clay surface of the courtyard. The bundles of wheat were spread on the ground, the flailers lined up at one end of the mass. Who could handle the flail more efficiently and reach the opposite end more quickly? The huskers sat around a pile of dry ears of corn. Who could husk more of them in a given time? Who had the necessary strength to husk the ones that weaker hands could not manage? I always bet on Father; and if he failed, I could produce a plausible excuse. But I don't remember that he ever failed. There was power in his arms and hands.

When the work was done, the courtyard was swept, we ate bread and cheese and *salame*. We drank wine. Then there was dancing to mandolin and accordion music. There was always someone skilled in reciting fables and legends. Thus, where work and play were so traditionally similar, the transition from the one to the other seemed perfectly natural.

As a peasant, Father was in some ways quite extraordinary among his peers. Most of them were illiterate; he had completed the second grade. Mother had not gone to school at all, but he had taught her to write her name. She did it well enough, slowly and laboriously, for it was a long name and difficult: Annunziata, the past participle of *annunziare*, to announce. But they were both very intelligent. She had served as a wet nurse in the home of a wealthy French family and was fluent in Parisian French. For that and certain other virtues acquired in that environment, she was more sophisticated than her husband, so their marriage was graced by a measure of equality and reciprocal respect not common among Casabianca peasantry.

In a home where there were no books or printed material of any kind, Father was privileged to borrow an occasional newspaper from a neighbor, a mechanic in a shop a few miles away, to which he traveled daily by bicycle. The mechanic's name was Silvio, and he had had what was probably the equivalent of a high school education. He also had some books, one of which was *Pinocchio*. Another was *La madre* by Grazia Deledda, a Nobel laureate. Silvio was fond of Father and made his limited library available to him; he also had a part in *Il testamento*. Thus Father was able to read in the evening in our home, and to comment on what he read to the family and the few neighbors who were interested.

He was judicious, reflective, even-tempered, not given to idle talk. He listened very carefully to any discussion of controversial issues that had substance, but he seldom participated. His reactions were facial: a raising of the brows, a slight smile, a pressing of the lips. However, when an appeal was addressed to him to settle differences, his invariable answer was, "Get the facts. Does Antonio raise more corn per acre than Pasquale? Does garlic planted in December keep better than what is planted in January? Has Barolo a longer life than Chianti? Alfredo and Giovanni disagree on the number of troops Garibaldi led against the Holy See? Loud voices and passion and insult are no answer to these questions. Get the facts." For these virtues he was called *l'avvocato*, the advocate. He was also a confirmed anticlerical.

In the home, at the table, or after dinner when he read aloud or was playing cards, or was the caller in the game bingo (called *tombola* in Italy), and he was not *in pensiero*, he was the life of the party. He had high culinary standards and insisted on the best we could afford. Mother was an excellent cook and could do wonders with the simplest raw materials. When he had properly sniffed a huge dish of pasta, he recited the secular grace, "*Pancia mia fatti capanna.*" Belly of mine, make a warehouse of yourself. Or, making a cruciform gesture with a slice of bread in his hand, he gave the benediction "*Nel nome del pane del salame e del vin buono*"—In the name of bread, salame, and good wine.

Mother atoned for his heresies by regular attendance at church and occasionally inviting the parish priest for dinner on Sunday. Don Camillo was rather more worldly than saintly. One Sunday, when Mother brought to the table a capon after the soup, and a huge quantity of cooked wild chicory, the priest uttered an observation that gave Father a chance to demonstrate his ready willingness to please our clerical guest. Don Camillo said, in effect, that peasants whom circumstances compelled to eat a lot of herbaceous and salutary vegetables such as wild chicory were lucky. "Right you are," said Father. "For your health we shall now put ours in jeopardy. You fill your belly with chicory; we will eat the capon."

Don Camillo laughed and said, "Please pass the bread." And Father, with a reverential bow and a majestic sweep of the hand, said, "Let the bread pass to Don Camillo." The bread, of course, did not move. Mother gently scolded Father, passed the bread to Don Camillo, and told him that he must not take Father too seriously. But he had made his point, and we proceeded with the dinner.

When he called the numbers for tombola, 1 to 90, he had a name for each: 33 was called as "the years of Christ," 45 as "halfway," 9 as "the eye with a tail." And when someone needed

occasionally recited, addressed to us as a command in good humor. I remember it for its jolly ring and certain words nice boys and girls did not use: "*Alto là! ruffian cretin bastardo pidocchioso!*" What ho, you filthy cretin lousy bastard! That was the first line in one of Father's speeches.

Among the things I have long regretted not having done during those early years was getting a copy of that folk drama. Father had it written on several sheets of paper, in a hand that might have been that of a teacher of penmanship. So I have but a vague idea of what the testament dealt with. Thinking back on the part I heard Father rehearse several times, I have concluded that it must have been a quarrel among several legatees of a disputed will.

Father had a copy of the entire drama, while each of the other actors had only his part. Hence the loss of the script, with all the necessary cues and stage directions, would be irreparable. Was it lost? Father kept it, as we all knew, in a drawer in the kitchen; and when he had gone to get it that morning, it wasn't there. Having asked all around and received a no with a shrug of the shoulders, he asked again. "Are you sure? I put it there Friday evening after rehearsal. No one but you has been in the house. I suppose it has simply walked away." He had, indeed, put it there. I had seen him do it. "Are you sure?" Again shrugging our shoulders, we looked at each other, puzzled, in fear.

"One of you is lying." That was the felony that placed us in his jurisdiction. The accusation was so unlike him that I, his firstborn son whom he was training to be his successor, stood there with fearful incredulity. Was this a nightmare?

His anger mounting, he delivered his ultimatum. When the

two minutes had passed, he removed his belt. Mother, gritting her teeth and with clenched fist, stepped forward from behind us. She grasped the belt, trying to take it from him. "My children do not lie, and you shall not do what you will regret."

While they were struggling for possession of the belt, my twelve-year-old sister, by now furious, gave the drawer such a yank that it fell with a clatter to the floor; and what was lost dropped on top of the drawer below it. The circumstantial evidence that had been all against us was now direct evidence against Father.

The drawer in which the text of the testament was placed had been packed with folded linen. To close the drawer after he had laid the script on top of the linen, Father had found it necessary to press with his hand on the sheets of paper. With the pressure removed and the drawer carefully closed, a slight upthrust of what had been forced down had pushed the script into the upper framework of the drawer; and when it was opened but not removed, the script remained where it could not be seen. My spunky sister's violent yank had dislodged it, and now the direct evidence was all against Father.

Father provided the above explanation in a happy postmortem. In that instant when the script was found as if by a miracle, he said nothing. Instead, with tears in his eyes, he tossed the belt in the fire grate. Thereafter he wore suspenders.

The material welfare of his family was constantly on Father's mind. In this respect he may have been a more worthy member of the human family than certain other Casabianca fathers. But the compelling reason was simply that in that place and at that time, a sharecropper, at the mercy of the landlord and the weather, was never certain of his daily bread. Where Father differed from others was that he was a peasant—cursed, shall I say? —with the tastes of an aristocrat. When Don Camillo reminded him that man does not live by bread alone, his prompt answer was, "Certainly not; he wants a steak with it."

What is eaten with bread in Italy, and invariably an inferior bread by peasants, is called *companatico*, from the Latin *cum panis*. In order to improve its quality, by making both plants and animals produce their most lucrative yield, Father did what Darwin, in formulating his theory of natural selection, had observed was the procedure of enlightened husbandry. The quality and quantity of plants and animals were improved by always using the best stock for reproduction. Improved and also, under certain conditions, varied.

Having noted the results of conscious selection by man, Darwin asked, "Can nature thus select?" And his answer was "Assuredly, she can." Father, of course, had not read Darwin; what he knew, he had learned by intelligent observation and experience. Thus he was able to take from the few acres, and the animals that were fed some of their produce, the most lucrative yield. The result of his intelligent husbandry added somewhat to our companatico. It wasn't much, because some of the yield had to be sold for the cash needed to buy necessities that could not be grown.

Soon after he had tossed the leather belt into the grate, Father began teaching me what he had learned. He was a gifted teacher, who taught with the patience that became a man who was wearing suspenders, and embellished the instruction with interesting commentaries. "Do you see these plants of cabbage?

Which is the best, the one we should keep for seed?" I looked at them carefully and chose the biggest. "You are right," he said, "but don't be impressed by mere bigness. Is Mother's brother, Modesto, a better man than I because he is much bigger? Is the big bumblebee better than the small honeybee? An artichoke the size of a lemon is much better, more tender, has less waste than one twice its size." I did not, of course, fully appreciate these differentiations; but Father certainly knew that a seed put in the ground today will bear fruit tomorrow.

He also taught me how to slaughter and skin a rabbit. "Grasp its hind legs with one hand and let it hang for a few seconds. When it stops squirming and raises its head with an upward arch of the neck, give it a hard blow at the base of the head with the other hand. Take careful aim. Do it quickly. Death must be instantaneous so the rabbit will not suffer."

These instructions where followed by a demonstration. "In skinning a rabbit, as in skinning a frog, we begin with the hind legs and simply remove their clothes. However, of a frog we chop off the head, while of a rabbit we carefully remove the skin. There is nothing edible in the head of a frog; but in the head of a rabbit, as in the head of a lamb, a calf, a pig, there is meat of excellent quality.

"When I was in the army, my colonel assigned me to the kitchen staff where the food of the officers was prepared. Nothing was lacking in that kitchen, and I have not eaten so well since. Once we slaughtered a dozen rabbits. Since the officers knew nothing about heads as a delicacy, the chef made a savory stew for them and we roasted the heads for ourselves. With all the necessary aromatics, plenty of olive oil and white wine, the result was a feast fit for kings. The tongue, the cheek, the eyes, the brain: therein is the concentrated excellence. Remember this, my man, when you take my place at the head of the table."

He also taught me how to kill a chicken. "The rich chop off the head; the poor know better. Take its head firmly in one hand, whirl the flapping creature around a couple of times until its neck breaks. Then suspend it by the legs. When it no longer flaps its wings, the precious blood shall have drained into the neck."

These instructions were also followed by a demonstration. One whirl by Father and the neck was broken. He quickly plucked the feathers and singed the body by holding it above a flaming handful of straw. Then he made an incision from the breastbone down through the anus, pulled out the entrails, opened and cleaned the gizzard, removed the bile sac from the liver. "Now," he said, "I am going to show you how to clean the intestines. These, too, the rich throw away. Some of them waste more than they use. The poor may envy the rich, but they learn nothing useful from them."

He slit the long coil of the intestines and drained off the excrement. Then, working carefully in several changes of water, he rinsed them until they were absolutely clean. The result was a cupful of precious flesh. Another salvaged delicacy.

Father occasionally took over the kitchen on Sunday, wearing a white shirt with sleeves rolled to the elbow and open at the throat. When soup and roast chicken were on the menu, he began by assembling the ingredients for the broth: beef shank, chicken head and neck, tip end of the wings, gizzard, legs, all the aromatics (carrot, celery, parsley, tomato, bay leaf, peppercorn, half an onion scorched to reduce its acidity and two cloves stuck in it). In preparing the chicken for the oven, he laved it with a mince of garlic, parsley, and sage stirred in a blend of olive oil and a bit of wine vinegar.

All of this was done early in the morning. Later, when the soup kettle was simmering and the bird was roasting, the aroma in the kitchen was enough to urge new life in the moribund. And I was there, Father's shadow, sniffing, observing, doing his bidding, unconsciously storing in the memory what I would do decades later when I too would be a father in his image.

For breakfast on Sunday after early Mass, he usually made a *francesina*, a "Frenchy." In a sprinkling of olive oil in the skillet, he barely warmed a few thin slices of prosciutto, overlaid them with sliced or crushed tomatoes, gave the skillet a brisk circular shake, then added as many eggs as were necessary, dropping each one carefully so that the yolk would remain intact. Covered with the lid for a couple of minutes until the eggs were set, the francesina was done.

Another dish that he prepared for breakfast or lunch when he had slaughtered a chicken was a sort of omelet. The cleaned intestines, which had been soaking in slightly salted water overnight, were thoroughly dried. Then he wrapped them carefully around green onions from which part of the leaves had been cut. These he braised in olive oil until they were lightly browned. The eggs for this dish were beaten together with some grated Parmesan cheese. If you want to know what culinary elegance you have been missing, try it. Or, better still, get a live chicken and start from scratch.

—*Father and Son*

DREAMING THE AMERICAN GOOD LIFE

WHAT KIND OF PEOPLE WOULD WE LIKE TO BE?

[*A speech to the University of Washington*
Medical Alumni Association, spring 1979.
A bottle of wine and a loaf of bread are on the podium.]

Macbeth: How does your patient, Doctor?

Doctor: Not so sick, my lord,
As she is troubled with thick-coming fancies
That keep her from her rest.

Macbeth: Cure her of that.
Canst thou not minister to a mind diseas'd,
Pluck from the memory a rooted sorrow,
Raze out the written troubles of the brain,
And with some sweet oblivious antidote,
Cleanse the stuff'd bosom of that perilous stuff
Which weighs upon the heart?

Doctor: Therein the patient must minister to himself.

Macbeth: Throw physic to the dogs; I'll none of it.
If thou couldst, Doctor, cast
The water of my land, find her disease
And purge it to a sound a pristine health,
I would applaud thee to the very echo
That should applaud again.

(From Shakespeare's *Macbeth*, Act V, Scene 3)

I have begun thus unceremoniously, reading lines from a tragedy familiar to you all, for two reasons: It seemed an effective strategy for diverting your attention from these puzzling and, given the time of day, appetizing exhibits, and concentrating it on me—five feet seven of a particular molecular sequence of carbon, hydrogen, oxygen, nitrogen, and phosphorous atoms; and epigenetically, the structural elaboration of an unstructured egg. And that I am, genotypically defined. However, phenotypically defined, I am what you see: five feet seven, a trim one hundred and sixty-five, a young lion, an unbridled colt of whom, my dear ladies, you must beware. For when I was an immigrant lad twelve years of age, in the Grays Harbor country, intent on beginning to sow my wild oats among the blond Nordic maidens in the New Land, a saintly teacher of Presbyterian allegiance and Scottish descent, warned me, having seen it in action, that the twinkle in my brown eyes would get me in a peck of trouble. It has. It still does. It always will. But oh, the honey-sweetness of that trouble.

Now then, should you be amazed at my phenotypical self, happy as the grass is green and blooming as the month of May, a prodigy whom age cannot wither nor custom stale its infinite variety; if, I say, you are amazed at what you see and yearn to learn the formula that has produced such a prodigy, you shall have it. In the ontogeny of the unstructured egg, the prime nutrients have been, since pre-natal days and with every dinner thereafter, the best of the staff of life and the finest of the Holy Blood of the grape. Therefore, I say to you aging Aesculapians and your mates; and especially to you as may be living in fear of being over the hill, and tempted to mutter with the melancholy Dane "O! that this too too solid flesh would melt, thaw, and resolve itself into a dew"—to you I say: a pox on such gloomy thoughts! Stock your cellars, improve your cuisine. And instead of putting money in your purse, put rosemary on your lamb chops, and grace the ingestion with good bread and fine wine. And a plague on sleeping pills! A tot of sherry when you retire and a heavenly choir will induce the innocent sleep, sleep that knits up the ravelled sleeve of care.

But enough of this scrupulously honest self-description, genotypically and phenotypically noted. It has served its purpose, though given to you with tongue-in-cheek braggadoccio. I want now to explain to you my second reason for having chosen to preface my remarks by reading a brief and familiar scene from a familiar tragedy. The embattled Self in that scene is in dire trouble. Its memory must be relieved of a rooted sorrow; the written troubles of the brain must be erased; its bosom must be cleansed of the perilous stuff that weighs upon the heart. In short, it must be purged of its morbidity and restored to a sound and pristine health. Hence the appeal to the doctor in obedience to the wise dictum drawn from Materia Medica: *venienti occurrite morbo*, oppose a distemper at its first approach.

I was reminded of that scene when I read the course objective stated on your program, and noted the subject of my colleagues' lectures; for the scene seemed to me an appropriate introduction to what those who planned this course for physicians hoped to accomplish. The objective of this course is to provide physicians and their spouses with new insight as to who they are and how they function in society in order to help them better live their lives. The assumption here is unmistakable. Pope was wrong when he said whatever is is right. All is not well with physicians and their spouses and, by a logical extension, with the rest of us. There is a malaise, a *morbo* in what is so glibly called these days "the human condition." I put it this way because the rest of us no less than you are in need of what the course assumes you lack, or do not have enough of: a knowledge of what you are in relation to the times in which you live and the world you inhabit. You don't know who you are as physicians, sexually, under stress, from the point of view of literature and history. Nor do you know what kind of people you would like to be. Hence, the general malaise, the *morbo*, the perilous stuff that weighs upon the heart. And to cleanse the stuffed bosom, you need, above all else, self-knowledge.

You may remember the Delphic oracle's injunction: know thyself; and you may remember Freud's revision of that injunction to read: to know thyself is to be known by another. Those who planned this program must have known that; for they have provided the necessary others by whom you shall come to know thyself. This, then, is a vast psychiatric ward, minus the Freudian couch for lack of funds. And that's a pity, for you are required to imagine yourselves prone upon it. Posture has been an essential strategy for all spiritual exercise; and Freud knew this. The prone position induces relaxation, passivity, receptivity, humility, and submission. Freud, however, who knew so much and probed so relentlessly the embattled self, only to conclude that he could do no more than lessen its endemic misery, did not know that wine is a relaxant. Fortunately, I who know so little, do know what the presiding deity of the brotherhood of Shrinkers did not know. So I have provided the wine. It is a bottle of Robert Mondavi Cabernet Sauvignon 1974. You are asked to imagine that you have it at your elbow. Take of it an imaginary sip, thus. Take another. And now that you are relaxed, receptive, submissive, and appropriately humble, lend me your ears; for I come not to bury the embattled self, not to decrease a little its misery, but to find its disease and purge it to a sound and pristine health. Abjuring drugs and surgery, I shall effect the purge by magic. However, in this thaumaturgical procedure, no less effective than your pharmaceutical, I shall need your aid; for you must remember the Doctor said, "Therein the patient must minister to himself." Grant me, then, your willing cooperation.

Imagine yourselves a Phoenix. You are being consumed by fire. Burn, burn with a gem-like flame the embattled Self. Leave not one molecule unconsumed. And now, abracadabra and hocus-pocus, arise from its ashes completely transformed. Transformed into what? Precisely into the kind of people we would like to be. However, since man does not exist *in vacuo*, since he is ineluctably an integral part of his total environment, we are now, by virtue of the so potent art of your Prospero, the kind of people we would like to be, living in the kind of world we are pleased to inhabit.

May I now attempt a brief profile of what we have miraculously become? We are men and women each of whom has an unambiguous identity and a will instructed by conscience endowed with certain rights and free to set a course teleologically determined and joyfully pursued; men and women who are not alienated from themselves, from their fellows, from nature. Restored to a sound and pristine health, our hearts and minds, our feeling and thinking, our faith and reason are in perfect harmony; dedicated to becoming something rather than on getting something — remember the rosemary on your lamb chops? We pledge all our efforts and our resources, for ourselves and our posterity, toward perfecting the arts of living. And the world that we inhabit is congenial to the realization of these ends.

Such is the vision of the kind of people we would like to be; and if we are not such people now, or if we are only partially, latently, potentially so, the reason is that we live in a world that is not congenial to the realization of our transformed selves. But even as we made the world what it is, we have the necessary genius and means to make it what it ought to be. Do we have the necessary will instructed by conscience? This entire program, the kind of inquiries it proposes, is evidence that we are groping our way toward such a resolution. And since we are unhappy with what we are, there must be causes for the malaise, the *morbo*, the alienation, the ambiguity, the pollution, the consumerism, the evisceration of the planet Earth, the strut and fret and strain of day by day existence.

The causes of this collective wretchedness are several; but there is one to which the others are ancillary: the prostitution of science in the service of a heartless technology. I hinted at the hegemony of science when I defined myself genotypically. We have come hither by deceptively seductive stages: the Renaissance, the Reformation, the Age of Enlightenment, the Age of Industrialization, the Gilded Age of the Robber Barons, the Atomic and Hydrogen Age. And where are we now? I shall give you the answer of an eminent scientist, the biochemist Erwin Chargaff: "Science has been operating under the Devil's doctrine. It says whatever can be done must be done—a doctrine that abolishes with one stroke all problems of conscience and free will. In the name of that doctrine, the two greatest technological misdeeds of our day, the atomic bomb and the landing on the moon, are certainly the children or at least the bastards of science. A single concrete example of the Devil's doctrine is what is vulgarly called genetic engineering. It is not so much that I fear success —there won't be any—but rather that each such attempt, windy and hopeless and barbaric as it may be, lifts our sciences and all of us to an even higher level of moral chaos."

The reference here is to those molecular biologists who are playing games with recombinant DNA, deoxyribonucleic acid. DNA is generally thought to specify the hereditary properties of the cell. In it are encoded all the characteristics of the cell that can be transmitted throughout the generations. By genetic recombination in the intestinal tract, the hope is the production of two Einsteins in every American home; but the irreversible consequence may be the production of little biological monsters.

Thus, we are about to—shall we say progress?—into the Age of Recombinant DNA, a venture which Chargaff and other eminent scientists oppose as an unconscionable assault on Nature. They also abjure and condemn with understandable bitterness the scientist's version of the Hippocratic oath, the Devil's doctrine that what can be done must be done. And where do I stand?

I lack the necessary knowledge to support or oppose that doctrine with authority. For I am, as some of you know, an amateur in the kitchen, the garden, and the cellar—the fellow next door who has written extensively on what constitutes the Good Life. However, I am also a teacher who abandoned the law for the humanities, and who has at long last reached the highest pinnacle in the academy, a status which a guard at one of its several gates called *E-me-ri-tus*, that mysterious disease of what are called the Golden Years. And as such, I am bound in conscience to declare with conviction and authority, borrowing a phrase from the hurly-burly of politics, that in the world of tomorrow, the Humanities must be given equal time with science. For if we are intent on becoming men and women in whom heart and mind, feeling and thought, faith and reason are in perfect balance, and living in a world congenial to the realization of this goal, we must balance the teaching of science with instruction in the arts of living; and particularly the art of living together.

The late Jean-Paul Sartre, having tortured his mind with a relentless search for the meaning of existence, having explored existentialism and Marxism, finally embraced such traditional values as hope, fraternity, the family, and democracy. In his last months he said: "Today, I consider that everything which occurs in one's consciousness in a given moment is necessarily tied to, often engendered by, the existence of others. What is real is the relationship between thee and me." I have known illiterate peasants who have lived by that credo. The educated brain, uninstructed by an educated heart and conscience can be a menace.

And now I am about done. I have said no more than you could reasonably expect from your little old wine maker in answer to the question: What kind of people would we like to be, living in a world congenial to the realization of that vision. Let us say that that is akin to Tennyson's far off divine event to which the whole creation moves. Far off but attainable, if we restructure our lives and reassess our values with that vision in mind.

Meanwhile we must live as best we can day by day, as we move toward that vision. In a lecture in New York at the time of the moon landing, unhappy that American feet had left their print on the dust of the moon, dubious that such a technological triumph would in any way improve the human condition, I concluded thus: The world is sick with too much brains. If we must probe the moon and outer space, let us balance that act of reason with an act of faith and probe the heart of our neighbor. Let us answer confrontations on the street with fellowship at the dinner table; and to counteract the venom of discord, let us pour the holy blood of the grape and eat together of the staff of life, symbols of communion, fellowship, and hospitality.

And now to you of the medical faculty, I shall make an unorthodox proposal: add to your curriculum a course on The Dinner Table as Prevention and Therapy. Ask me to conduct it and require it of all your students. A few months ago I suggested to our governor that she should add to her staff a chef and wine steward, reminding her that the great Talleyrand won his diplomatic victories with the resources of his kitchen and his cellar. To the offer of my services there has been no reply; and that is why matters in Olympia have been getting gloomier and gloomier.

In order to whet your appetite for lunch, let me describe a

115

notable dinner prepared by Rosa Mondavi, Robert's mother, in her kitchen and with my assistance. In the fall of 1968, at the height of the vintage season, the air permeated with the aroma of crushed grapes, on a Saturday afternoon, Rosa and I fashioned 950 ravioli. The filling was a composite of veal, pork, chicken, calf's brains, herbs and spices. The enfolding pasta was made with semolina and eggs. The savory sauce was enriched with game birds from the vineyard. The roast was venison; the mushrooms were *Boletus* from the Mayacamas hills, the wine was vintage Cabernet from her private cellar, the abundant bread had been baked the preceding day in her oven.

The preparation of that dinner was a labor of love, made the more so by frequent sips of a noble Zinfandel, and punctuated with jovial remembrances of things past in the Old Country. There were fourteen of us at the table, all immigrants or children of immigrants, enjoying with never-ending gratitude the bounty of the New Land. None had ever heard the words alienation and the human condition. No one referred to the wine with such words as fruity, full-bodied, nicely balanced. Occasionally one of us caught another's eye, lifted the glass, winked, sipped, and smacked the lips. No sophisticated word monger could have praised the wine more eloquently.

Rosa was in her late seventies, a grand, spirited Mother figure full of the joy of life, irrepressible, indefatigable. In the performance of a Mother's various labors, I have seldom seen such capable hands as hers. In her way of life, as the old Church Fathers used to say, *Laborare est orare*. Labor is a form of worship.

After dinner we danced the tarantella. And then we slept. No pills. No tranquilizers. No soda for sour stomachs. The dinner table as prevention and therapy.

Once more I direct your attention to these symbols. In the leavened loaf there is strength; in the bottle of wine there is gaiety. Let us look to our kitchens and stock our cellars. Call friends and family to the dinner table. Salute each other with beaded bubbles winking at the brim and purple stained mouth. Act now. Pull the cork. Don't hesitate. We've nothing to lose but boredom and despair.

THE INITIAL CHALLENGE

WHAT IS THE American dream? Is it to rise from log cabin origins to the White House? From a desk to the president of the corporation? From poverty to wealth? From obscurity to professional distinction? Or is it a more modest dream—to have congenial employment, a happy family, and own one's own home? By the end of the recently celebrated bicentennial, many of these goals had been achieved by the millions who had come to America during the two preceding centuries. Since most had been drawn hither by the promise implicit in America's fabulous natural endowment, it was inevitable that they should conceive the American dream in economic terms. But economic gain has no more than marginal relevance to my vision of the dream.

Anyone who has more than an elementary knowledge of American history will agree that there are two American dreams: the collective and the individual. The collective dream was, initially, the enduring hope that the nation would progress in accordance with the "truths, ends, and purposes" set forth in the Declaration of Independence and the Constitution, especially its preamble and the Bill of Rights.

As for the individual dream: its content—that which one dreams of and seeks to gain—is highly personal; the right to the dream, with the realistic hope of gaining what one seeks, is the supreme heritage, transmitted from generation to generation, of every American citizen. This legacy is structured in our democracy. When Jefferson, in writing the Declaration of Independence, substituted "the pursuit of happiness" for Locke's word "property" in listing a person's inalienable rights, the right to the dream became a part of the fundamental law.

During the first two centuries after the founding fathers had established the new nation, the dream, as one of economic gain, was realized with relative ease by those who were shrewd, aggressive, and richly endowed with the acquisitive instinct; and it was during these decades that the nation's endowment—land —was up for grabs. Thereafter, when what was left of the total natural endowment was largely in the domain of private enterprise and when the growth of monopolies had reduced the effectiveness of competition and the plenitude of general op-- portunities, there was a tendency, for the first time in our history, to become skeptical about the American dream as one of economic gain. It was no longer possible, for example, to do what Rockefeller had done. At sixteen years of age he began work as a clerk. At age twenty-four he invested three thousand dollars in an oil refinery; and at age forty he owned ninety percent of the nation's oil refineries. This was symbolic of what could be dreamed of and achieved during that period in our economic history when so much was available to anyone whose talent and temperament were congenial to that sort of quest.

Similarly, about six decades later, when my generation graduated from college in the middle twenties, opportunities for employment or for venturing into one's own enterprise were virtually unlimited. When the agents of higher education had come to urge our high school senior class to go to college, they sought to persuade us by a single argument: the more education you have, the greater will be your income. Commencement speakers made the same promise, along with certain pieties that no one took seriously. The sequel proved them prophetic. For while we worked toward a college degree, we had the assurance that our studies were an apprenticeship in the real life course we would follow thereafter. Nor were we disappointed; when we graduated, and had had a much needed rest after years of laborious study, each one of us proceeded to the workplace that the logic of the times had made available to us. Those who had chosen to continue their studies in graduate school were welcomed by the dean with no questions asked—an undergraduate degree was the only requirement. Not so today.

Forty years later, when my son graduated from the university, employment opportunities were severely limited. He, with a degree in romance languages, and one of his friends, with a degree in philosophy, could find no employment, so they did what had probably never been done before. Using their backgrounds in humanistic studies to lure salmon into their nets, they earned their bread as commercial fishermen in Bristol Bay. It was rumored that their extraordinary success prompted others in the fishing fleet seeking to increase their catch to return to school and earn a degree in liberal arts.

What, then, of the dream in our and future generations? Is

it myth or reality? Such dreams as Rockefeller indulged in are now out of the question. Considering the continuing depletion of the planet's major resource systems, wisdom requires us to dream of ways of conserving rather than exploiting what remains of our natural endowment. This is not only a matter of declared national policy, but it ought also to be the concern of every individual. One who, in his personal design for living, avoids waste, extravagance, conspicuous consumption — quite independently of what the community may require — is a true conservationist. One who owns a plot of ground, adds to its natural fertility, and keeps it productive, helps to maintain, even by ever so little, the nation's cornucopia. One who plants a tree of a rare variety, or who gathers seeds of certain flora and provides for their germination and development is reducing the number of species that are in danger of extinction. These are dreams that increase self-respect because they embody what is right and proper and, though they require little of the dreamer, they add enormously to the general welfare.

There is current evidence, for those whose goal it is to rise from the log cabin (that is, from humble origins) to political or other eminence, that such opportunities are still a reality. The governors of our two most populous states, several senators, a score or more congressmen, and hundreds of others who have achieved eminence in business and the professions are children of immigrants who had little or no education and who began life as common laborers. Their gift to the new land was the talent and intelligence lodged in their genes, and those who were capable of dreaming, and who lived long enough, would see the dream realized in their children. Imagine, for example, the felicity that must grace the golden years of the parents of Mario Cuomo, governor of New York.

As I said above, economic gain is of no more than marginal relevance to my conception of the dream. The opportunity to earn one's bread, yes. That is a condition precedent to all else. Beyond that, the American Dream, properly conceived, is the inalienable right to seek happiness in self-realization. A just society, the overall goal of which is to promote the general welfare, says, in effect, to each of its members: Know thyself. Discover as early as possible your talent, your highest potential and within the framework of that self-knowledge, set a course, pursue it with vigor and imagination so that you may realize what was latent in your inborn physical and spiritual endowments. Where you need legitimate aid in your quest, society will provide it. And always remember that in your design for living the welfare of others is no less important than your own.

Bearing this in mind, I suggest that we forget about economic gain and concentrate on becoming something—the best that is latent in us. The dream, thus conceived, is and always has been a reality. The more we insist on the dream as an inalienable right and pursue it with determination, the more likely it will be to remain a live option available to all. For ultimately it derives from us, the people, and, as a community working together and intent on the same ends, we are, at any moment in our history, more likely to be what we had intended to become than to be something else. With that vision always in focus, every advance we make may very well lead to another and every realization of the dream will engender another.

—*American Dream*

TOWARD
HUMANE LIVING

AMERICA!

"Land of coal and iron! land of gold! land of cotton, sugar, rice! Land of wheat, beef, pork! land of wool and hemp! land of the apple and the grape! Land of the pastoral plains, the grass-fields of the world...."

Since Walt Whitman sounded his barbaric yawp over the rooftops of the world, the American landscape has undergone considerable change. The pastoral plains have been impoverished; many of the forests have been denuded; much of the subterranean treasure has been wastefully extracted. The builders of the nation, bold and reckless and impatient, have indeed used the body of America a little irreverently.

And yet, in an exhausted world, America remains the land of plenty. It is no exaggeration to say that the agricultural possibilities are relatively unlimited; while technological discoveries may postpone indefinitely the exhaustion of materials basic in the nation's economy. From every possible point of view, the opportunities yet latent in these blessed states are the envy of the less fortunate millions of the earth. An immediate and urgent problem for the American of today is how to use them toward humane living.

Needless to say, the problem is not a simple one, and the suggestions that might be made are many and varied. I have deliberately limited myself to exploring the significance of bread and wine, and the activities and attitudes that they imply, as constituents in humane living, partly because they are of basic importance, and partly because they are so frequently neglected. Because of an abiding conviction that the life of an immigrant can be fundamentally instructive to his American fellows, I have chosen to write from the detached point of view of one of them who has tried to absorb the best in the culture of America without losing what is valuable in his own. This conviction I have felt with such compelling honesty that the temptation to go beyond the limited theme of this book has not been, I fear, entirely resisted.

Of course, I am not so naive as to suggest that one may find in these pages the complete formula for a contented life. Before the conditions to human welfare become equally accessible to all, there are persistent problems in politics, economics, and social relationships which must be solved by intelligent, collective action. These are matters with which the American must preoccupy himself as a citizen. But regardless of the age or the environment in which he lives, the individual cannot escape a residuum of indivisible responsibility for the attainment of his own happiness. Where the conditions to his well-being are contingent, he must act as a citizen; but where they are purely a matter of his own will and initiative, he must bestir himself as an individual.

There is much that he can do to give his leisure hours a creatively significant content. I have emphasized activities and attitudes that seem to me most frequently neglected sources of felicity. Implicit in the various anecdotes relating to the experience of the immigrant, and in all the trivia about bread and wine, is the simple lesson that the home is the appropriate place where man may realize some part of his dignity. Temperance and imagination in the nourishment of the body are homely virtues which may be achieved with ever increasing joy. A sane economy in the administration of domestic affairs should be an attribute of all men regardless of their circumstances. Resourcefulness and self-reliance in providing for the family's immediate needs are ancestral values which one should strive to rediscover. The pursuit of these ends will yield a measure of contentment of which no man should deprive himself.

The emphasis which I have placed on food and drink may need some elucidation. The cuisine may be generally regarded as a part of a people's culture. The quality of the fare, the manner in which it is prepared, the time devoted to its ingestion, the conventions of the dinner table: these are intimately related to, and frequently reflect, a people's esthetic development. The Europeans and the Asiatics have developed their traditional cuisine by utilizing in the highest possible degree the resources peculiar to their time and place. Across the centuries and by imperceptible degrees, they have made it an integral part of their culture.

The American, lacking the spur of necessity and engrossed in the exploitation of resources with which no other nation has been blessed in anything like the same degree, has been understandably satisfied to feed on plain meat and potatoes. His curiosity about culinary matters, of relatively recent origin, is an encouraging sign. If he would proceed wisely, however, he must remember that the evolution of a traditional cuisine requires time. His immediate concern should be a willingness to experiment, an insistence upon quality, a purging of his mind of all culinary prejudice, and the development of a humane attitude toward the dinner hour. These, and not a slavish imitation of foreign recipes and esoteric menus, are the bases upon which a sound American cuisine may be eventually developed.

He must also guard himself against a danger to which he is predisposed by his esthetic naïveté: the tendency to be easily impressed by cults and coteries of foreign descent. The culinary poseurs, foreign and domestic alike, are out to capitalize on American credulity in cultural matters. Their insistence that cooking is an art, and eating and drinking a ritual, has thrown the dinner hour out of focus and produced needless confusion. There are few Americans, for example, who can serve a dinner which deviates a little from the native tradition without being somewhat self-conscious about it. And who is certain about when to serve red and when to serve white wine? The proper attitude, of course, is that it doesn't make a damned bit of difference.

I have emphasized bread and wine as ingredients in the good life, for a further reason. As an immigrant, the discovery of abundance has been the most palpable and the most impressive of my discoveries in America. Nothing so much as this fact has brought home to me the spectacular contrast between my old home and my new. I have sought to communicate the personal significance of this fact to my fellow Americans in the hope that it may awaken them to a more keen realization of their heritage and make them aware of their responsibility in preserving the nation's resources for the children of tomorrow.

As the years pass and I become more and more identified with my new home, this initial discovery remains an important clue to the meaning of America. I have observed, for example, that in his attitude toward food the American reveals significant aspects of his character. The endemic waste, the exclusive reliance upon the grocer and the butcher for all his culinary needs, the obliviousness to what grows freely in the environment—do not these reflect his indifference to frugality as a virtue, and his subservience to what I have called the quantitative fallacy? Where the game everywhere played is for high stakes, there is no understandable value in any bend of effort unless its relevance to some large undertaking is immediately perceptible. Frugality in itself, the prudent use of Nature's gifts, is meaningless. In a land that idolizes the Rockefellers and the Fords, the growing of a carrot and a cabbage seems a trifling preoccupation—unless, perhaps, they can be exhibited as the *biggest* carrot and the *biggest* cabbage ever grown anywhere.

There is yet no evidence that the experience of the war years has had the salutary effect for which some of us had hoped. The American still wastes and continues to trample underfoot whatever does not measure up to his gigantic illusions. He does not yet perceive the consequences of having used with reckless imprudence the precious yield of the good earth; he does not realize that the quantitative analysis of value is fundamentally deceptive; nor does he yet see with any clarity that, in his uncritical devotion to big things, he has neglected the trifles which, in their totality, constitute a principal ingredient in human happiness.

I should not be at all hesitant to say that, of the principal ingredients, it is the most important, and that this book may therefore be properly regarded as a continuous emphasis on neglected trifles: the garden, the cellar, the simple pleasures of the dinner hour, a scrupulous husbandry in the home, the quiet joy of modest achievement. These are all phases of what ought to be one of man's central preoccupations—the attempt to discover within his own domain the felicity he cannot find in the market place.

I am perfectly aware that I am insisting upon old-fashioned virtues, and that there is a touch of agrarian décor in the inducements I am offering my fellows to join me in eccentric anachronisms. And that, of course, is precisely my intention. The best and the wisest of men—oh, certainly there have been exceptions!—have found solace within the garden gate. "God Almighty," said Bacon, "first planted a garden; and, indeed, it is the purest of human pleasures; it is the greatest refreshment to the spirits of man; without which buildings and palaces are but gross handiworks; and a man shall ever see that, when ages grow to civility and elegance, man comes to build stately, sooner than to garden finely; as if gardening were the greater perfection."

The bleak winter months have passed, and the earth is relaxing under the incipient sun. Beneath the kitchen window, the wild violet is in bloom, the azalea, the tulip, and the daffodil are swelling with life. The chicory planted in the fall is sending succulent shoots through the softening crust of the ground. The first green onions will soon be ready for the table. Bleached and hidden in the mulch, the dandelion is waiting for the frugal element. The sap is rising in the peach tree and the blush of life is visible in its buds.

Each morning, before I set out for the classroom, I walk leisurely through my diminutive estate. As Charles Lamb, at his home in Edmonton, "watched with interest the progress toward maturity of his Windsor pears and jargonelles," so I delight in the first flowers and survey in anticipated pleasure the tender shoots of leafy delicacies that I shall have with my evening meal.

I know that my butcher, who serves me so well, will have my favorite cut of meat when I shall call at his shop at the end of the day's work. What will it be? A roast? A steak? Sweetbreads? Lamb kidneys? Whatever the choice, it will be prepared with care and served with the appropriate vegetable from the garden.

Before dinner there will be the customary descent down the cellar stairs, with the infant gourmet at my heels, into the cubicle of Temperance. I will see there a sight familiar enough: shelves stocked with last year's produce from the garden; mushrooms from the meadows and the hills; seafood from the waters of Puget Sound; bottles of red and white wine of various ages; and the cradled oak barrels in which last year's vintage is "breathing through the wood." A sight familiar enough! But always evocative, pleasantly reassuring, and mildly exciting.

It is not an inadequate symbol of the fusion of two cultures. What I have called the cubicle of Temperance reflects the tangible results of the immigrant's thrift, his industry and resourcefulness, his high culinary standards, and his instinct for humane living, when these have found scope in the prodigality of the American environment. Mere trifles? Of course! But they can be transmuted into the indispensable means to a better life.

—*The Unprejudiced Palate*

FAMILY

ANGELA IN THE GARDEN

Wᴀᴛ ɪ ᴛʀᴀɴꜱᴍɪᴛᴛᴇᴅ to Angela, our first child, best reflects the familial modes I have pursued in teaching children and grandchildren the things my father used to do. We were then living in a smaller house, and the kitchen garden was a plot twenty by forty feet. It was a Sunday early in May 1939. She was four years old. The bright sun was already warm at eight in the morning. When I had shaved and drunk a first cup of coffee, I went to her room to awaken her for breakfast. At my first call she opened her eyes, yawned, stretched, rubbed her eyes, sat up in bed, and asked, "Father, what the hell do we do today—I mean, what work in the garden?" And I said, "Yesterday we spaded; today we shall plant beans—limas and Romani and Blue Lakes. So you had better get up and put on your boots and coveralls."

She sprang out of bed and dressed herself and came to me to lace her boots. Then we sat down to a breakfast of pancakes, sausage, eggs, coffee laced with brandy.

"Yesterday," I told her, "when I spaded, you were somewhere between a hindrance and a help. You must do better today or I shall get another helper."

"Yes," she said, "today I shall help all the day."

So we drained our cups and went to the garden plot, she with her sandpile bucket and I with rake and shovel. I raked the spaded ground and leveled it and staked out the bean hills and dug the holes for the seeds. She carried the manure in her little bucket and dropped it in the holes, and when I had drawn some soil over it, she dropped the bean seeds there, six to every hill. Indefatigable as an ant, with beads of sweat like tiny pearls upon her forehead, her tongue pressed between her teeth, she trudged back and forth from the manure pile to the raked plot of ground, carrying the bucket in front of her, supported against her thighs, the handle gripped firmly by both hands.

For three hours we labored together. When the work was done, and the family's supply of beans for the coming year was assured, she asked once more: "And now what do we do?"

"And now," I said, "we shall sprinkle ourselves with the garden hose and wash away the dirt and the sweat; then we shall go to the cellar, where there are red and white wines and goat cheese from Battistoni's goat ranch in the Black Diamond hills." "I want red wine," she said. "You may choose the bottle you want," I said, "then we shall sit in the cellar astride a barrel and, as we nibble cheese and sip wine, I shall tell you the fearful story of the anthropophagous monster, Piripicchio, and the Isle of Desires. Would you like that?"

"Goodygoodygoody! Let's hurry!"

We hurried. We sprinkled ourselves with the garden hose and washed away the dirt and the sweat; and when we had dried ourselves and put on clean clothing, we went to the kitchen for glasses and bread, then descended the cellar stairs. The bottle she chose was a rich, robust red—I have forgotten the pedigree. I wiped the neck of the bottle and pulled the cork, while she held the two glasses and pranced a little in joyous expectation. When I had poured the wine and tasted it and found it good, we sat astride a barrel and sipped the wine and nibbled the cheese and munched the bread. And I told her the story. When the story was over, she began to drowse. I took her in my arms and carried her to her bed, in the nursery, at the east end of the house, high above the garden plot where we had spent the morning together planting beans.

The sun had now passed over the roof and it was cool. I drew a blanket over her and bent down to put a kiss on her forehead. Her breath, drawn slowly and evenly, smelled of cheese and bread and wine. How ineffably just, that the breath of my little girl, who had helped me with the spring planting, should smell of bread and cheese and wine! These had been the three basic foods in my childhood and of my peasant ancestors. How often, in the late afternoon—teatime in the city—in the shade of some tree, after hours of working on the land, as she had worked this morning, I had had a sliver of cheese, a chunk of bread, and a draught of wine, the sustenance that should carry me through to dusk and to supper!

And here we were now, father and child, a generation and a world removed from the anxious days of my childhood, unwittingly merging past and present in the joy of bread and wine and cheese after labor on the land. I stood at her bedside in the wonder of it and in silent admiration. She had worked so hard and so willingly and had literally earned her bread in the sweat of her brow! Beautiful maiden, full of spunk! What a Mother you are fated to be! Lucky the man who shall have you as a mate!

—*Father and Son*

WINE AND CHILDREN

I ATTENDED THE birth of each child and the first two grandchildren—the other three were born where I could not be present—with a bottle of my best wine. When the nurse had prepared the infant for the mother's breast, I dipped the thoroughly scrubbed index finger of my right hand in the wine and traced it across the child's lips. Why the right hand? Because it was the right thing to do. Then I poured a glass for the mother, to sanitize her alimentary canal and hasten the flow of milk.

As fact and symbol, the ritual celebrated the birth. Thereafter, I set aside magnums of the best wine made in my cellar to celebrate the tenth and twentieth birthdays of children and grandchildren. I chose the one date because it was on the threshold of puberty, and the other because it was the beginning of adulthood. Meanwhile I did what was necessary from time to time to teach them that, according to my ancestral tradition, bread and wine are the staff of life; that the one makes the heart strong and the other makes it glad, that wine is the symbol of hospitality and the appropriate beverage with which to celebrate dear occasions.

Since we celebrated so many such in our home, and always poured a glass of wine for our visitors, the children and grandchildren learned all of this by the way.

I also taught them how to pour wine, swirl it in the glass, note its viscosity, sniff it before sipping it slowly to engage the taste buds on the palate and thus complete the organoleptic test.

I taught them also, and my wife as well, the difference between a good and a bad wine, a new wine and one that had been aged several years in the bottle. The ones now in their twenties and older, having assisted in the cellar work for several years, from crushing the grapes to bottling the wine after it has been in oak barrels for two years, are acquainted with the procedure in making a superior wine. They have anticipated the vintage season with pleasure and enjoyed inviting their friends to participate in the bacchanalian rites. One look at the grapes when they are delivered from the vineyard, and the most attentive know whether the wine will be ordinary or superior.

Occasionally, and without telling them, I have tested their knowledge of wine at the dinner table, being careful of course to make the test a reasonable one. Once I served them a wine that was two years old and told them it was five years old. My wife immediately noticed the deception. The others agreed with her. Had I made a mistake, taken a bottle from the wrong bin? No. Then I told them that the professor was testing his students. Had I served them a wine that was four years old and told them that it was seven, would they have passed the test? I doubt it. Would I have passed it? I doubt it. The difference between the two would be nearly imperceptible.

When our first grandson was born, I began immediately to

educate his nose and palate in both wine and food. I told him that certain dishes have a pleasant odor, that wine has a bouquet, and that it is proper to sniff what one eats and drinks. Once, when he was three and a half years old, he had dinner with me and my wife. We had pork chops aromatized with garlic and fresh sage. The wine was a fine cabernet. There was a small stem glass for him, into which his measure of wine would be poured if he asked for it. He knew, as did our children when they were very young, that he would be given wine if he asked for it. He did; and I poured him enough to half fill his glass.

My wife, who was never persuaded that a child so young should have any wine at all, surreptitiously added a bit of water to it while he was sniffing his pork chops. After he had swallowed his first bite of the meat and bread, he took the glass, looked at the wine, sniffed it dubiously, looked at it again. "What kind of wine is this?" he asked. "It's a pink wine," my wife said. He looked at the color, sniffed once more, and took a sip. Then, addressing the grandmother, he said, "You put water in it; I like my wine plain."

What assurance! What inferences! How courteous the reproach! When we celebrated his tenth birthday he invited the guests, all adults, poured the wine from the magnum that had been reserved for the occasion, took his place at the head of the table, and proposed the appropriate toast: *Salute!* His name was Thomas Reese Owens, son of our eldest daughter, Angela, and Tom Owens, of Pittsburgh, Amherst, and Michigan law school. Now in his middle twenties, the precocious wine connoisseur is coaching a professional football team in Finland, having been a running back on the football team of Pomona College. He is a big man, and sniffs his food and wine in a way that befits a man of such a size.

I also taught the children and grandchildren to lace their morning café au lait with brandy—what my father called grappa —and to dunk toasted and buttered homemade bread in it. To lace, I say, not to spike it, for the intent is to improve its taste. My father did it, I do it regularly for breakfast, and so do some of them, especially our son and Thomas Reese.

The result of these instructions has been precisely what I intended: that in the art of living they should follow the Hellenic rather than the Puritan mode, moderation rather than abstention. What I did for Thomas Reese, and later for his sister, Sarah, I had done also for our children. Their knowledge of wine excels that of their peers, in whose homes wine was not the appropriate dinner beverage. They prefer it to liquor, know their measure, pour their own at the dinner table, and participate in whatever comments may be provoked by a given vintage.

My father believed that what was proper for him to drink was also proper for the children, always in a measure appropriate to their years. Since I share that belief, there has never been even a hint in our home that children are forbidden to drink some of the beverages the parents drink. Thus they have never found it necessary to deceive us; and we are fairly certain that they will remain, as they are now, invulnerable to the kind of overindulgence that places family and life in jeopardy.

—*Father and Son*

FORTY-FIFTH ANNIVERSARY

CERTAIN EVENTS IN the past are remembered for an evil that must not be repeated, or celebrated for a good that they engendered. In the evolution of our society, Pearl Harbor is an instance of the one, and the Fourth of July, 1776, an instance of the other. And thus it is in the evolution of private lives.

Intelligent, sensitive, ethical men and women who have committed grave errors remember them to the end that they may not be repeated; while they celebrate in a variety of ways and with a feeling of profound gratitude the anniversary of such events as made the pursuit of happiness a meaningful and creative quest.

A marriage may or may not have been such an event.

When it was not, when it engendered nothing but wretchedness and was later repudiated, it is remembered as an error that must not be made again. When it was the beginning of an enduring happiness, its various anniversaries are appropriately commemorated.

However, in a society where wedding anniversaries are traditionally celebrated, it is well to note a distinction between such as are celebrated as a matter of form, and such as are celebrated as a matter of substance.

In the one case, the celebrants merely conform to custom, doing what convention expects; in the other, they do what the heart requires.

By its very nature, the celebration of a wedding anniversary, when the event is ceremoniously remembered for the sustained happiness it engendered and the children that were teleologically conceived and nurtured in love, is strictly a family affair. Its meaning, what partakes of sacredness in it, is lodged in the hearts of the happily wedded couple and of their issue. Hence it may be considered in bad taste to make of that meaning a public expectation.

However, if there are elements in the celebration, in the means chosen to commemorate the anniversary which the celebrants feel others may find richly suggestive, an account of it addressed to the community may be justified on social and ethical grounds.

And since the anniversary of which I propose to give an account may be properly considered to be of this sort, I do so hoping that the reader will not find it in bad taste.

If our society is threatened by moral crisis, surely the current obsession with sex, manifested in promiscuous cohabitation particularly among the very young, the alarming increase in the dissolution of marriages for petty reasons, the ill-considered irrelevance of the marriage ceremony, the alienation of the children from their parents, and the consequent disintegration of the traditional family—surely these are some of its salient manifestations.

These disturbing phenomena may be transitory; they may

be the effect of certain imperfections, grave errors in the way we have ordered our lives; and as such, they may be an unavoidable interlude along the way toward a clearer vision of the familial and social values they deny. Let us hope that this is so.

Meanwhile, let us miss no opportunity to keep this vision before us.

My wife and I were approaching our 45th wedding anniversary. Aware of the disturbing phenomena mentioned above, blessed with children whose exemplary filial piety has been a main source of our happiness, and since we were well into the "golden years," we decided that on our anniversary we would celebrate not our marriage but 45 years of family solidarity.

And we decided to do it in such a way that the children would be the principal beneficiaries of the celebration.

How could this be done? How could we celebrate family solidarity and what they had contributed to its integrity? Finding the appropriate means required neither ingenuity nor guesswork. The children often had said how marvelous it would be for the entire family to visit the place of my birth. It had been their dream, enjoyed as such in the fancy. For the village where I was born was in another country some 8,000 miles away.

But the dream was kept alive; and now, after 45 years of marriage, we were in a position to risk bankruptcy and make it come true. So we invited them to come as our guests for a three weeks' anniversary celebration in Italy. We were six.

The impulse was generous; and since a generous impulse should always be immediately translated into action, we emptied the piggy bank, bought tickets, reserved lodgings in Florence; and before the pauser, reason, could chill the emotion, we were airborne to London, thence to Milan and on to Florence by rental car.

Our son, Brent, a match for any dare-devil Italian at the wheel, was our driver. The drive to Florence, 180 miles to the south, across the lush valley of the Po River, over the Tuscan Apennines; our first dinner together at the pensione, followed by a chamber-music concert, set the tone for the entire three weeks holiday: pleasure and harmony unlimited.

The weather was fair and warm. In the compact auto, none bigger available, we fitted tightly, elbow to elbow, thigh to thigh, bottom to bottom. Its condition was such as to provoke nothing but collective anxiety expressed in humorous quips.

Would it get us there? Of course it would.

It was a Fiat; and fiat means "Let it be done."

And so it was.

However, the auto was a terminal case; and the next evening it was dead. Parked on a street scheduled to be washed after midnight, it had to be moved to avoid having it towed away by the police. We pushed it across Lungarno, a street where the traffic was heavy and furious, up an incline and onto a bridge across the Arno River. It was a risky and difficult maneuver, accomplished without the offer of aid of Italian motorists hell bent on getting there from here.

The next morning the agency provided a "new" auto, a battered Fiat mini-bus—adequate vehicles were simply not available—that was only metaphorically new. It served us well enough on that day; grudgingly, but well enough.

On the morrow, we were invited to lunch by our friends, Jim and Joan Hogg, at their summer home 20 miles up in the hills above Florence.

Giving ourselves plenty of time, we boarded the bus at 10 o'clock. Gay as the month of May, once more in tight togetherness, we cried out:

"Let's go!"

Brent leaned forward, turned on the ignition. The battery was dead! We called the agency, and a mechanic appeared an hour later with a new battery. But he couldn't remove the old. A burly fellow with powerful arms, he swore, he sweated, he tugged, he scratched his head. The frozen corpse would not budge. *Pazienza!*

He returned to the shop for more effective tools. Now armed with heavy hammer and crow bar, he removed the battery piece by piece; and at 12 o'clock we were on our way.

We had stood in the scorching sun for two hours, in the din, whine, and explosions of furious traffic, a severe test of one's patience, an occasion for an excusable grouch or gripe or flare of temper.

But there was none of that. Our collective reaction was jocular quips punctuated with laughter; for we had a tacit understanding, immutable because tacit, that we would permit nothing to blemish our celebration of 45 years of family solidarity.

And nothing did.

The children proposed spontaneous toasts to the parents and the parents responded in kind. Whatever we did, we did together; and the tight togetherness in the Fiat was at once real and symbolic. Pleasure and harmony unlimited.

Since our three weeks' holiday was in the nature of a family pilgrimage to the village of my birth, there had to be a ceremonial focus in the various things we did together. A dinner in one of the fine restaurants of Florence would not be the appropriate means. I wanted something in harmony with my peasant origins in that village and with our modest way of life.

Accordingly, I planned a *merenda*, a late-afternoon snack, a sort of coffee break which as peasants we took in the fields after long hours of labor and before a late supper.

On the anniversary date we drove to Casabianca, visited the church where my birth and baptism were registered; and in an adjacent field we shared bread and wine, cheese and salame. I had also procured a bottle of champagne, as a symbol of the increment to my well being, which had been the consequence of my immigration to the opulent Pacific Northwest.

And with that bubbly wine I proposed a toast to 45 years of family solidarity, at once a private and a social virtue rooted in antiquity. The intention was to proclaim an imperative for the future by commemorating what had been achieved in the past; for family solidarity is seldom achieved without effort.

And thus that simple ceremony with bread and wine, itself of ancient lineage, with its social and ethical implications, was established as the focus of the many things we did as a family.

And when we returned to our homes in America, the blessed land that had provided the necessary piggy bank for the three weeks' commemorative holiday, we were united in remembering the journey, gay and flawless from the beginning to the end, as the finest and most creative venture we had ever undertaken as a family.

Fiat!

—*The Seattle Times*

BUONGUSTAIO

SENSE OF SMELL

I~N LATE SEPTEMBER~ 1949, my wife and I were walking along the ancient Appian Way, a few miles from the Coliseum in Rome, enjoying the *campagna*, loitering in the shade of the pines, observing the ruins of tombs and monuments which reflected the historic antiquity of the landscape. It was a fair day, with not even the whisper of a breeze as the sun began its decline on the western horizon.

The long walk had given edge to our appetite; and as we paced ourselves along the lengthening shadows of the pines, we compared our preferences for the dinner we would have at the Trattoria di Righetto: Stracciatella? Saltimbocca? Ossobuco? Scaloppine? Salivating with anticipation, we moved along briskly, as my nose, trained from infancy to sniff, told me, in so many sniffs, that we were approaching the source of a strangely seductive culinary smell. Illusory? Successive sniffs confirmed the smell's reality. And yet, where was its source?

Off to our right, several hundred yards away, was what appeared to be a monastery. Surely the fragrance of food in preparation for the table could not reach us from that distance.

However, it had lodged in our nostrils from somewhere, and its authenticity was unmistakable. The source could not be far away. Immediately ahead of us, on our left and adjacent to the road, was a tomb in partial ruin, a structure of thick walls, about four yards square. At the top the walls were truncated, as if by an explosion. Since there was no other building in sight, that ruin must be a residence and its occupant must be preparing dinner. My wife agreed and we trotted toward it.

As we followed our nose thither, I remembered a somewhat similar experience recorded by an Italian painter and amateur chef in Florence:

My father loved good food and he had a cook who could provide it. His name was Angiolino. When I was a boy and enjoyed what he cooked I frequently visited him in the kitchen. Impressed by my boyish interest in his art, he gave me some elementary cooking lessons, let me smell what he was preparing. Years later, when I was established in my own studio and he had long since left my father's house, I was walking along a back street permeated by a familiar culinary odor. Following my nose I came upon him standing in the entrance to his kitchen. An old man now and I did not recognize him, but joyfully cried out his name: Angiolino! It was he; and the fragrance of his cuisine had brought me to him!

The ruin was what we expected, and its address was 249 Via Appia Antica. It had an opening as for a door and another as for a window. I peeked in and saw a lady stirring a skillet. Greeted as if I had been expected, I was invited in and she told me her name, Signora Coscia. There were seven children; her husband was in a sanatorium. Victims of the war, they were waiting for the government to provide them living quarters.

Never mind the distressing details of that ruin's interior. My habitual sniffing is about to reveal to you a perfect example of natural simplicity in cookery, the essential doctrine of this book by Alice Waters and Paul Bertolli, as opposed to refinement, sophistication, and rigid formulas. But first a word about odor, the sense of smell, and of taste, its corollary.

The eminent medical scientist and brilliant essayist Lewis Thomas has noted that "we might fairly gauge the future of biological science by estimating the time it will take to reach a complete, comprehensive understanding of odor." No doubt it will. Meanwhile, let us educate the nose by constant practice. In the kitchen it is an indispensable aid in testing the olfactory correctness of, let us say, a broth, a sauce; while an appropriate sniff at the table will add to the pleasure which the palate will derive from what is ingested. Furthermore, and more to the point, the pleasure in reading the vivid, appetizing descriptions of food in preparation given in this book will be enhanced by engaging the nose in the learning process, precisely what I have done.

The sensitivity of one's nose and palate can be easily improved by repeated smelling and tasting. But it may be more difficult for some people to develop a taste and olfactory memory, to remember the smell and taste of, let us say, a glass of wine drunk months ago, or recall a smell in its absence. Since my father began training me to sniff when I was a child, a training I have passed on to my children, I can recall at will, for example, the smell of frogs cooked in a tomato sauce flavored with *puleggio* (*Mentha pulegium*), last eaten when I was a boy in Italy. I tested my memory of this in our kitchen when I had found puleggio and repeated the recipe substituting catfish for frogs. Perhaps you have had a similar experience. At any rate, it is worth the effort to cultivate these faculties, since their use is so important in the kitchen, at the table, and in sniffing, shall we say, the landscape along the Via Appia Antica.

As soon as I had smelled what Signora Coscia was stirring in her skillet, my nose told me what she herself confirmed: wild mushrooms. She and her children had gathered them early that morning. They were now being sautéed in olive oil, garlic, parsley, and *nepitella*, colloquially called *erba da funghi*, mushroom grass, the appropriate herb for mushrooms. I knew immediately what was in the skillet, for I had cooked wild mushrooms in precisely the same way hundreds of times in our kitchen in Seattle. Nepitella grows wild in certain regions in Italy, and when one buys mushrooms there, a few sprigs of the herb are included in the purchase.

Could there be a more perfect example of natural simplicity in cookery than wild mushrooms, freshly gathered and immediately cooked as described above, using the indispensable herb also freshly taken from the soil? Prime raw materials with the appropriate condiment, such is a basic premise of this book. Elsewhere I have written that herbs are the soul of cookery— fresh herbs. And the wise restaurateur, intent on excellence, will know where to find them. In a small restaurant in London, I was so elated when I was served oven-roasted potatoes aromatized with fresh rosemary that I consulted the manager. He took me to the storage room and showed me chests of the indispensable ones. Fresh rosemary and other herbs in an unpretentious restaurant in London! And, of course, at Chez Panisse in Berkeley.

The best book on the cuisine of Italy was written about half a century ago by an amateur: *L'arte di mangiar bene*, the art of eating well, by Pellegrino Artusi. "Select prime raw materials from the two kingdoms of nature and respect their integrity in the kitchen." Such is his basic culinary principle. This book, for which I am delighted to write the introduction, is Artusi brought up to date gastronomically. I have given you an example of natural simplicity in cookery; here is another from my own kitchen: Leeks organically grown, and using only the bleached white portion, are split lengthwise, braised in butter, and given a sacramental drop or two of balsamic vinegar. Amen.

Alice Waters and Paul Bertolli in the kitchen illustrate an Italian proverbial saying: *Sono come il pane e cacio*. They go together like bread and cheese. They complement and inspire each other; where one plans, the other executes. Drawing from their individual culinary experience, each contributes to this masterpiece of gastronomy that which reflects that experience. Homemade pasta in pasta country is an art taught to young girls practically from infancy. We are given the result of such training in the brief essay on basic pasta by Alice Waters:

Making pasta is a simple process of combining flour with egg and water and kneading the mass to an elastic consistency. This can be done mechanically or by hand. I am partial to the hand method as it allows for the most control. The cook is always aware of the feeling of the dough, develops a sensitivity and understanding of the variables involved. There is really no substitute for the hands-on technique.

Precisely! When an Italian cook in London was asked why his pasta was the best, he spread his capable hands and said, "*Ah! Ci vol quella man.*" It requires that hand. And when an aging baker was asked why he did not use a mechanical mixer, his reply was that when he could no longer mix with his hands he would quit baking. Alice Waters is of that estimable breed; and so she does the pasta section.

The section on risotto is the work of Paul Bertolli. It is introduced by a brief essay on that justly famous northern Italian dish, which can be prepared in a number of different ways. The most typical of these is saffron risotto; all others are variations on that theme. "This risotto," Paul says,

represents my fondest and most vivid childhood memory of food. It is associated with holidays, particularly Thanksgiving and Christmas, and was prepared by my grandmother. Until I traveled to Italy, risotto always meant one thing—to my child's eye, an enormous cauldron of golden rice and the mingled fragrance of saffron, poultry broth, butter and parmesan cheese. To me this was the most delicious food imaginable; and when

I left home I sought to recreate the taste I so remembered. Of course, I repeatedly questioned my grandmother about the ingredients and the process involved,
but her instructions were sketchy, as is always the case
with Italian grandmothers when asked to give a recipe.
Nevertheless, enticed with some new bit of information she supplied about salt pork, or dry porcini mushrooms, or the kind and quality of broth, I continued
to try to make her risotto.... Although nothing can
supplant the taste memory of that dish, I am perhaps
closer than I have ever been to recreating it.

With the taste memory as guide and inspiration, and his
own innate culinary talent, Paul not only re-creates, but enlarges
on what he remembers. Hence the classic variations on the basic theme which follow the introductory remarks. Each variation
is composed of several ingredients which combine to produce
what the authors call "a harmonious whole." This is precisely the
result sought in the preparation of all composite dishes. Artusi
calls it an amalgam of flavors.

And what does this mean in terms of the nose and kitchen
procedure? Give the nose a peach and it smells the odor that
emanates from it; add to it a strawberry and a liqueur and it
records a bouquet. When I recall the frog dish, I do not smell
frog, puleggio, or the several other ingredients; I smell the harmonious whole.

The kitchen procedure which produces it is roughly scien-
tific. There is the hunch in the mind of the cook, the intuitive
guess that if A is done, B will follow. Hence the hypothesis. Then

the experimental verification. In other words, the creative cook, drawing from his knowledge of the raw materials of the two kingdoms of nature, imagines the harmonious whole that will result when certain ones are combined in the preparation of a dish. Sound procedure. As an example, note how Alice Waters created what she calls a "rabbit salad."

Such is the metaphysics of the culinary art: reasoning in the kitchen from what is known about prime raw materials to that which one intends to extract from them, a harmonious whole, a cuisine of natural simplicity purged of refinement and rigid formulas. Doctrinally inspired, well written, this book is an encompassing variety of culinary preparations, designed to satisfy man's innate desire for that which is pleasant and for an explanation. Accordingly, Alice and Paul provide an enlightening reason for the ingredients and the procedure they have chosen in preparing a composite dish. And it is, of course, an important feature of this inspired book on the culinary art; for the amateur must be taught not only how to prepare a given dish but also why he must do it in a certain way. That is sound pedagogy in the kitchen as well as in the classroom.

And now that I have given you a hint of what this remarkable book contains, if you are of the breed who mind their stomach very carefully and very studiously, you will want to read it with utmost care. Do so and engage your nose in the learning process; for as you sniff your way from one appetizing recipe to another, the book will be your Via Appia Antica, with Waters-Bertolli stirring the skillet instead of Signora Coscia. Read and enjoy what I am pleased to recommend. Pleased and privileged.

—from the foreword to Chez Panisse Cooking

A SLIGHT
TOUCH OF
HERESY

W E HAD JUST won the game that gave us the Coast Conference championship in football. Bill's parents had left that morning to spend the weekend at their cottage on Puget Sound, and we were to have the house to ourselves. What an opportunity to stage a jolly undergraduate brawl! Would I prepare the dinner?

Why not? Had I any experience in cooking? No. Would I know how to proceed? Why, of course. All Italians can sing. All Italians can cook. All Italians can. . . .

Bill was amazed at my confidence—and somewhat worried, for we had invited, among others, a favorite professor of philosophy who was a practicing gourmet and of whom we were in considerable awe.

I had not, until then, undertaken anything more ambitious than frying an egg. And yet, I must confess my confidence was genuine. Without hesitation I proceeded with the shopping. My selection of a rabbit—mildly shocking to Bill and the girls—was an almost instinctive choice. At home, that animal had been more or less traditional fare for the Sunday dinner. Except for the artichokes, which occasioned some bewilderment, the other items on the menu were less uncommon and therefore more reassuring to my friends.

I said I had had no experience in cooking. Well, that is only a partial truth; for I had always lived in a delightfully culinary atmosphere and had served, so to speak, an unconscious apprenticeship in the kitchen. How often had I dressed a rabbit, or assisted Father with the task, on Saturday afternoon! How often had I gone to the garden, at Mother's bidding, to get a sprig of thyme, a bit of rosemary, a little parsley, as she salted and peppered the rabbit and laved it in olive oil preparatory to roasting it! And ho! the number of times I had minced herbs under Mother's occasionally impatient scrutiny!

Without actually being aware of it I had absorbed considerable culinary skill—had become something of a cook before I had attempted to cook anything at all. As I prepared the rabbit for the roaster, I remembered without effort a procedure that I must have unwittingly observed a thousand times. I rubbed the rabbit with garlic, salted and peppered it thoroughly, and stuffed the visceral cavity with a variety of herbs taken from the garden of an Italian acquaintance. I asked Bill for some olive oil—without success. But I had seen the article for sale in drugstores, so I asked to see the medicine cabinet. Here it was, flanked by iodine and listerine! Bill told me his mother rubbed it on her scalp. He wasn't quite sure.

I poured it into the roaster and on the rabbit. While the

little animal was sizzling in the oven, I cleaned and halved the artichokes, a task I had reluctantly performed hundreds of times. I minced a little garlic and parsley which I worked into the artichokes after they had blanched for a few minutes. At the proper time I put them in the pan with the rabbit and basted them carefully with the oil, which by that time had been enriched with the meat juice.

Frankly, I do not remember whether the result even approached Mother's roast rabbit. The occasion was extraordinarily gay, thanks to an excellent wine provided by an Italian friend. The procedure and menu were sufficiently unorthodox to disarm bright western undergraduates who were hell-bent on emancipation from all traces of provincialism. I also remember having pitched their expectations rather high with the announcement that the dish had been a favorite of the sumptuous Borgias, and that all Florentines—including myself—prepare it with enviable skill. (I have learned since that even a pretty fair gourmet can be conditioned to make the proper response.)

Well! the food must have been rather good than bad. The professor was eloquent in his expressions of praise and quite metaphysical in his analysis of the flavor. He used such words as "essence," "synthesis," "substance"; and unless my memory fails me, at one point in his verbal exuberance he used the word "universal" in referring to the rabbit. To an immigrant boy who was just learning his way around at the University, the professor's performance was very impressive. What a pity that I had eaten roast rabbit so many times without enjoying its metaphysical subtleties! When dinner was over I was certain of one thing: the *particular* rabbit that I had prepared was consumed to the last morsel.

To that dinner, conceived in student gaiety and executed in utter innocence, may be traced a myth that, on occasion, has caused me considerable embarrassment. It was immediately bruited abroad that I was a chef of extraordinary resources, and that in the preparation of certain dishes I utilized the culinary secrets of the Borgias. Homes and apartments were placed at my disposal if only I would prepare a dinner for "a very select group." During the ensuing year I repeated the rabbit dish—I didn't dare attempt anything else!—forty or fifty times. Meanwhile I was trying desperately to live up to a reputation for which, I felt honestly, there was absolutely no foundation— except, possibly, a certain naïveté in my exceedingly enlightened friends. I systematized all the culinary knowledge that I had unconsciously absorbed as a reluctant apprentice in Mother's kitchen. I pestered with questions whoever I had reason to believe knew something about cookery. In short, I settled down more or less seriously—mostly less—to expand my sphere of culinary achievements.

The amiable professor of philosophy became my most effective press agent. As the years went by we became intimate friends. I cooked for him frequently and made his wine. When he went to meetings of philosophical societies, from coast to coast, he boasted to his astute colleagues that a vintner's son from the Chianti hills was in charge of his cellar. On at least one occasion he tucked the proof in his briefcase and went across the continent to read a brilliant paper in defense of hedonism.

For reasons that will be discovered on the pages that follow, I am suspicious of gourmets and connoisseurs, and so I resent being numbered among them. If someone suggests that I have "the artist's touch" in cookery, I swear that I shall feed him pork and beans with tinned spaghetti for dessert.

But despite my protestations, the myth that I am a chef has persisted. For the past several years my good friends have urged me to establish a restaurant. The more enthusiastic among them have suggested that I write a cookbook. The idea of becoming a restaurateur is wholly repugnant. The suggestion that I write a cookbook presupposes that I am either a cook or—heaven forbid!—a slavish plagiarist of untried recipes and perpetuator of culinary nonsense.

I love good food—as who does not? I take some pride in the fact that in the realm of gastronomy an unprejudiced palate is my only guide. Where I can't find food that pleases me, I fall to in the kitchen and prepare my own. Necessity has been the mother of what measure of invention and resourcefulness I possess in culinary matters. On occasion I produce something that smacks of real achievement. But I am not a cook. For example: I have never made an aspic salad, nor baked a pie.

However, the idea of writing a cookbook, after it had been suggested for a number of years, began to be somewhat alluring. Why not give it a try? An afternoon in my study, planning the chapters and writing out recipes, convinced me that the task would be unbearably dull. But perhaps I wasn't going at it in the right manner. So I spent the next few days examining critically the more popular, chatty volumes on cookery. It was during that time that I conceived the idea for the pages that follow.

Some of the books I examined are honest, pedestrian, unimaginative; some—very few—are honest and excellent.

Others are coy, incredibly naïve little volumes that proclaim on every page in prose that repeatedly misses fire, the Oh-isn't-it-fun-to-eat philosophy. The most offensive, and in some cases the most popular, are those inspired by an unassimilated foreign cuisine. These are phony, impractical, misleading, and decadent. All of them—excepting the honest few—give the impression of being commercially inspired, designed to attract that remnant of the population that has not yet outlived the synthetic Bohemianism of the twenties. I concluded that what America needs is not another cookbook, but a book on bread and wine in relation to life.

What is the labored theme on the pages of these exuberant volumes? It is implicit in each of them that American cuisine is monotonously mediocre and by all odds the worst among civilized peoples—a generalization that leaves much to be desired by way of accuracy. Every one of these precious books on food is an imperative to the American housewife to clear her culinary affairs with Moscow, Shanghai, Rome, Berlin, and, preferably, Paris. The nod toward Paris is definitely in the imperative mood. So far as I know, no one has been sufficiently smug and reactionary to suggest that American cuisine is potentially the best, and that in certain quarters of this sprawling republic, American cookery is right in there pitching in the *cordon bleu* league. But of this, more anon.

It would be folly to deny that in general the American cook has much to learn from his Latin, Nordic, and Asiatic fellow in the realm of pots and pans; or that every labor-bent peasant who crosses the terrifying Atlantic could add appreciably to the gaiety of the American executive's dinner hour. The difficulty is that those who have undertaken to teach the new world the culinary tricks of the old either do not understand, or consciously pervert, the meaning of bread and wine as ingredients in the good life. They are an articulate group—the exceptions are as rare as they are precious—of gastronomic adolescents who see this troubled life in terms of exotic sauces and unavailable vintages. Death to them is not the end of Life but the everlasting impossibility of smacking the lips and patting the bloated stomach. They may be wiser. On the basis of what they write on food and drink they are the "Lost Generation" among kitchen knaves. They constitute *The Decadent Cult of Cookery.*

The American housewife who would venture beyond the limited orbit of tinned foods and watery pot roasts must seek her guide among this coterie of culinary expatriates. Their gastronomic Baedekers, potbellied and in chef's bonnet—the function of which, incidentally, is to keep dandruff and hair from falling into the soup—confront her in every bookstall in the nation. They have been prepared with synthetic urbanity by provincial Americans whose knowledge of food is essentially bookish and painfully self-conscious; by hack writers and tenth-rate novelists turned gourmets for the nonce to contribute their bit to the gaiety of the American dinner hour. From time to time their ranks are invaded by foreigners of questionable antecedents who, eager to do anything but honest work, capitalize on American naïveté by writing about the food and drink that, in another clime, sustained their useless lives.

No doubt they are all contributing something to America's gastronomic coming of age; but what little good they have done is offset by an evil from which at the moment no release is in sight, unless this revolt is effective beyond the writer's most unreasonable expectations. They have broadcast a dastardly falsehood, perhaps to give a certain status to their labor of love—that cooking is an *art*. The implication of all their dithyrambic spewings on culinary matters, despite their protestations to the contrary, is that excellent food and drink are achievements in refinement beyond the attainment of ordinary mortals. Some write in a mystic vein, and, with phony reverence—certainly with a disgustingly disproportionate sense of values—of little Burgundian villages where, one would suppose, people do nothing but eat and drink and exchange notes on the latest truffle hunt. They recall with appropriate drooling, and in atrocious prose, *cordon bleu* cooks (one must not say "blue ribbon," since it smacks of prize bulls at county fairs and so would break the incantation!) discovered in this or that cranny of the Alsatian countryside. With incredible impracticability they write of meats which marinate a fortnight and then simmer and seethe for hours and hours. Their recipes, fantastic enumerations of exotic ingredients bathed in quantities of cream and blends of liqueurs, are designed to frighten the most adventurous bride into eternal allegiance to ham and eggs.

Their unintended success in this is a sort of poetic justice. The American housewife has been convinced by these culinary fakirs that cooking is an art, and since she is at the moment in full revolt against the thesis that woman's place is in the home, she is quite willing to admit that her cooking isn't worth a damn —despite the spherical tendencies of her own and her mate's girth. She is in no mood to achieve distinction in the kitchen if to do so she must go snouting for truffles in the oak groves of

Piedmont and preying upon snails in the vineyards of Burgundy.
If cooking is an art, then by definition it can be mastered only
by a select few—a conclusion which she has been quick to seize
upon and to exploit in defense of her admitted ineptitude. If
excellent meals require exotic and unavailable ingredients, endless hours in the kitchen, and a lifetime to perfect, Mrs. Jones is
content to whet the can opener and concentrate on bridge.

But she cannot consistently ignore the call to culinary self-
improvement. To meet special occasions she will now and then
hazard an invasion of the sacred precincts. After a hectic shopping tour through the foreign sections, where she has discovered
that many of the ingredients she had hoped to find flourish only
between the covers of the cookery books she has been reading,
she advances gaily into the kitchen and takes a snort of this or
that—whichever she happens to have on hand—to bolster her
morale and quicken the imagination. A survey of her pots and
pans reveals that they are woefully inadequate. Quaking with a
sense of impending failure, she begins to mince and sauté,
simmer and strain. Her nerves kept in perfect equilibrium by her
favorite cigarette, she meets each crisis as it emerges. Well in
advance of the dinner hour, each little culinary symphony has
received the final blessing, and the casseroles gurgle all over the
stove. The guests arrive, and after such appropriate exclamations
as "Oh, boy, am *I* hungry!" and "Doesn't something smell simply divine!" they light their cigarettes and settle down to guzzle
quantities of whiskey and soda. When their palates are properly anesthetized they crowd around the dinner table and, amid
laughter and corny ribaldry, stab uncertainly at the laden dishes.
No one says a damned thing about the food—a fact which Mrs.

Jones doesn't particularly notice, since she has done some pretty fair guzzling on her own account. But the morrow brings sober reflection—not to be confused with "emotion remembered in tranquillity"—and a reaffirmation of faith in watery pot roast, tinned string beans, and aspic salad.

—*The Unprejudiced Palate*

THE MYSTIQUE
OF WINE

"I N WINE TALK and wine tasting, there is an enormous amount of humbug and a great deal of pretense." I have forgotten who made this statement; but accept it as a fact and be wary of connoisseurs, especially the scribbling sort, whose attitude toward wine is one of awesome veneration, and who have conferred upon it a mythical status. Such solemnity is utterly ridiculous; and not infrequently it is a self-serving posture designed to set the connoisseur apart from the ordinary wine drinker who takes his wine in stride, as he takes his bread. It is understandable and most appropriate that such serious writers as Hemingway and Steinbeck should pay their respects to wine by referring to it as "one of the most beautiful things in life," and as the "Holy Blood of the grape." Some such metaphor would do justice to certain others of Nature's gifts intended for the palate and the stomach.

But note some of the solemn absurdities recorded by the scribblers. It has been alleged that a certain wine was so venerable that, to do it justice, an entire gourmet dinner had to be built around it; that a certain other was such an elixir that it had to be taken in reverent sips from a silver chalice; that a great Chablis is the only appropriate wine to drink with oysters. How can anyone who has not taken leave of his wits fail to laugh at such pretensions! And how about you? Are you not ashamed, humbled, humiliated, for having floated fried oysters to your stomach on hearty draughts of the most ordinary table wine? Certainly not! Possibly, when, as a wine drinker you were still in your salad days, you might have been humbled by such a reproach; but now that you are a wise old peasant with purpled feet and purple-stained mouth, you are unimpressed. And properly so.

For now you understand that bread and wine are twins; that either without the other is but half itself. You are so sensibly aware of this gastronomic truth that, even if you were pinned to the wall, you could not honestly say which is more important on a dinner table blessed with plenty of both. You know, also, that bread and wine vary in quality. Furthermore, with your knowledge of grape species, and as a competent winemaker, you can account for the degrees of excellence in wine, a competence and a knowledge ordinary wine scribblers are not likely to have. So, who is a connoisseur?

A good question. If the word refers to one who can distinguish a very good from an indifferent wine, then there are millions of wine drinkers who qualify as connoisseurs. But the word means more than that, for it is descriptive of a person with "informed and astute discrimination," especially concerning the arts and matters of taste. How many are thus endowed? By definition, very few. In the realm of food and wine, what feats of informed and astute discrimination establish the connoisseur's authority?

Here the scribblers record some amazing instances. It has been alleged that a French connoisseur of food could tell whether a trout had been caught upstream or downstream from a certain bridge on the Seine, and name every ingredient of the sauce in which it was cooked. Not at all a shabby performance! And even less so that of certain connoisseurs of wine who, after a sniff and a sip of a given wine, could deduce its quality, variety, age, and place of origin. And again: Two such connoisseurs, competing for supremacy, drew wine from a barrel and proceeded to judgment. The one identified it, gave its age, place of origin, and pronounced it perfect but for a slight defect: There was a trace of metal in it. The other agreed; but he detected a further blemish: The wine had a ropy aftertaste. And he emerged the victor, for when the barrel was emptied, a key was found in its bottom. And attached to it was a length of household twine.

Another feat of incredibly difficult discriminatory judgment was as follows: An unusually endowed connoisseur, given a glass of wine, was asked to name what it reminded him of. After a sniff and a sip he said: "Urine." Then, as if to underscore the sensitivity of his nose and palate, he added: "Yes! The urine of a duchess." Since one cannot identify that which he has not previously known, one wonders how often he had sniffed the waste expelled from the bladder of—was it his Last Duchess?

Such improbable feats as here recorded are drawn from the mystique, the mythology of wine. And so are certain words and phrases which are intended to be descriptive of wines, but which tend to mystify the ordinary wine drinker: imperious, balanced, flinty, foxy, having a consoling feminine aftertaste, velvety, harmonious, fruity, resembling bottled sunshine. It's no wonder that wine drinkers in America, intent on learning about wine, tend to approach it with regrettable diffidence. Since they cannot discern such subtleties in it, they either parrot the glib connoisseurs or conclude that they themselves lack the sensitivity of nose and palate necessary to appreciate wine's sublime virtues.

And that attitude, I say, is regrettable; anyone with an unstuffed nose and a normal palate and some experience in drinking wine, though not able to give them a name, can appreciate its sublime virtues. This I have proved to my complete satisfaction. On many occasions I have given such men and women a glass of great and one of an ordinary wine, without telling them which was which; and invariably they have raved about the one and dismissed the other with a shrug of the shoulders. These were intelligent, though not necessarily learned, and unbiased individuals eager to learn more about wine. On the other hand, an affluent disciple of the mystique coterie, and therefore something of a snob, proclaimed that only French wines were fit to drink; and that a certain California Cabernet was hogwash. In a blind tasting of two very good French and two California Cabernets, he chose the hogwash. Perhaps his palate prevailed over his bias.

So much for humbug, pretense, and misplaced veneration in wine talk and wine tasting. I want now to examine what measure of truth there is in the statement that after a sniff and a sip, a connoisseur can deduce the quality, variety, age, and place of origin of a given wine. Can it be done? Taking the statement as it stands, the answer is no. Properly qualified, the answer is yes. The wine to be thus identified must have an ascertainable identity; and the governing logic of such a test requires that the connoisseur should have had antecedent knowledge of it. For how can one identify that which he has not previously known? A further fact to consider in this context is that only a precious few wines have an identifiable character. The ordinary wines of America and Europe, the least expensive or moderately priced varietals, in jugs or in bottles, are generally made from grapes grown in different vineyards and so standardized in production that they have no identity, no individuality. For these reasons, such wines cannot be identified by anyone.

Bearing these qualifications in mind, let us give the connoisseur a glass of genuine Cabernet, one of equally genuine Pinot Noir and a third glass of genuine Zinfandel. Will he be able to identify the Cabernet and the Pinot? Most certainly, provided he has had considerable previous sensory knowledge of those two varieties; and most certainly not if he lacked such knowledge. Such a test would be relatively simple for a qualified judge. More difficult would be one that required him to give the age of the two wines; but he could do it, provided that some time in the past he had tasted the two vintages, noted the date, and had a good taste memory. It would be extremely difficult, if not impossible, if he were required to do what a wine snob bet he could do at a dinner party recorded in Roald Dahl's short story "Taste."

The host announced that the dinner wine was a great vintage Bordeaux. The bottle had been opened an hour ago so that the bouquet, long imprisoned in the bottle, might have time to come alive before the wine was poured into the tulip-shaped glasses on the table. The maid would fetch the wine from the pantry at the proper time. The guest, a glib, self-appointed connoisseur of Bordeaux wines, bet that he could identify it. The terms of the wager were set, the bottle, enfolded in a linen napkin, was brought to the table, and the mystery wine was poured, each glass half full. In serving great vintages especially, that is the proper amount, for before taking the first sip, one swishes the wine in the glass in order to admire its color and note the so-called tears, the wine's viscosity and oiliness, which fall slowly down the side of the glass after the rotating swish. The more or less ceremonial gesture also aids the bouquet's rise to the expectant nostrils.

Having performed this preliminary maneuver, the guest sniffed the wine and took a first sip. What he proposed to do would severely tax the resources of the most accomplished connoisseur, for in Bordeaux there are a dozen or so top wineries, known in the trade as *châteaux*, as well as many lesser ones. Had he tasted wines from all of them, including the one on the table? Did he have the necessary taste and olfactory memory to distinguish the one on the table from all the rest? As he proceeded in his analysis, he displayed an enormous amount of book knowledge of Bordeaux wines. That is, he knew the recorded characteristics of the various *châteaux*: Margaux, Haut-Brion, Lafitte, and the rest. He had in mind, also, words and phrases used by competent connoisseurs to describe the most famous *châteaux*. Thus armed, he began his dazzling performance.

Cautiously sniffing and sipping, he eliminated the *châteaux* in the St. Émilion and Graves districts, giving his reasons for the elimination. Therefore, the wine must be from the Médoc. He sniffed and sipped once more, closed his eyes, pondered, and was certain. Sniffing victory, he eliminated Margaux and Pauillac. Why? The wine to be identified lacked the violent bouquet of the one and the imperious character of the other. Furthermore, it had a consoling, feminine aftertaste. Once again he searched his memory and remembered that such consoling femininity was found only in the wines of the St. Julien commune. He knew now that he was on target; and the host began to fear that he would lose the wager. But since there were several *châteaux* in that district, the guest might not hit upon the right one. However, methodically stating his reasons with uncanny accuracy—wine dilettantes have such a store of book knowledge of wine!—the guest eliminated all but two: Chateau Talbot and Chateau Branaire-Ducru, 1934. Another sniff, another sip, another concentrated effort to remember, and he ruled out Talbot. And the host congratulated the winner.

The winner? Just a moment, mine host! While the guest was crowing modestly and moaning over the difficulty of his performance, the maid brought him his spectacles. He had left them in the pantry after he had examined the bottle of wine.

And this concludes the account of pretense and humbuggery in wine scribblings and wine tasting. It seemed to me an appropriate conclusion to the pleasure of advising the amateur winemaker, for it is fitting that you should know something about the nontechnical wine "literature" in which certain absurdities are recorded; know within what limits one may qualify as a wine connoisseur; and know that to identify a given vintage wine—its age and place of origin—in a line-up of wines, one must have had a previous sensory experience of it. The cheating by the guest in the story simply underscores the extreme difficulty, if not the impossibility, implicit in doing what he pretended to do, as the example I am about to give underscores the ease with which such an identification may be made in a totally different set of circumstances, by the ordinary wine drinker.

I have in my cellar two Cabernets. The grapes for the one came from the Napa Valley and for the other, from the Santa Clara Valley. The one is two years older than the other; and though of equal excellence, they are perceptibly different. People who have been drinking wine regularly for several years, having sniffed and tasted them until they were certain that they knew each one, given a blind test immediately thereafter, had no difficulty whatever in identifying them. Could they identify them in a line-up of Cabernets two or three years later? Possibly, if they had the necessary taste memory. I, myself, when the younger wine was some years older, and the difference between them was more subtle, could not easily distinguish one from the other. And this simply means that when the difference between two wines is not substantial, only an experienced wine drinker with a very sensitive nose and palate can discern that difference.

In conclusion, let us abide by certain fundamentals: Bread and wine of excellent quality are complementary on the dinner table; the one strengthens the heart, the other makes it gay. Let us respect them for what each does and strive to have the best of both. There are indifferent wines, good wines, superior wines. And the experienced wine drinker who can discern the degrees of excellence in wine, and never fails to recognize a good wine, is the genuine connoisseur—with no apologies to the esoteric fraternity. William James once said that the social value of the college-bred person consists in his knowing a good man when he meets one. Similarly, a wine connoisseur is one who knows a good wine when he drinks one.

—*Lean Years, Happy Years*

MEADOWLARKS

But for some succulent meadowlarks fattened in the wheat fields of the West, I might have married a farmer's daughter and inherited a wheat ranch. We were classmates in college. I had met her, appropriately, as a "worthy opponent" in an inter-club debate on the campus. When the brawl was over—an amazingly articulate chatter on installment buying, the economics of which I do not understand to this day—I joined the judges in conceding her the victory. I still suspect that their decision was based on reasons as noble as my own; for she was a blonde madonna, structurally flawless, and with a fine distribution of weight where weight is most appreciated on the female figure. No one could have resisted her argument the moment she unfolded it as she arose from her chair.

We had met as adversaries, but we soon became intimate friends. Then the fatal meadowlarks intervened and I lost a patrimony. She had often hinted that I might find her parents rather "different," and that they would likely consider me somewhat "strange," an observation which seemed to me wholly irrelevant, since I had absolutely no designs on *them*. Furthermore, I had just read Milton, Shelley, and Walt Whitman, who had added to my innate independence and filled me with the spirit of revolt. When it became rather obvious that we were behaving as if our future were to be a never-ending series of happy breakfasts together, she invited me to spend a week at the ranch in September.

I accepted eagerly, and late on a Saturday evening I arrived at what might have been my future home. Since I had been told that birds were plentiful in the wheat country, I had brought with me a slingshot, a weapon I had learned to use in Italy with uncommon accuracy. What I should have brought was a book on how to win friends and influence rich farmers, or at least an awareness of the vast gulf that separates Shelley from the opulent and insulated American rancher.

Our first breakfast together left much to be desired in the way of felicity. The food was extraordinarily good, the morning air and bucolic surroundings had given edge to the appetite, and both had inspired me to "strange" behavior. There were large eggs that had been dropped by the hens early that morning, thick slices of home-cured ham, wheat cakes made with sour cream, a pot of excellent coffee, and a variety of fruits and preserves. I went after the food as Samson had turned on the Philistines— and, I fear, with the same weapon. I took it in the nostrils; I smacked my lips; I gurgled and sighed. I took from my pocket a little flagon of liqueur and poured it into the coffee. Then I burst into poetry: "And bread I broke with you was more than bread." My blonde madonna twittered and smiled as she glanced from me to her parents, as if to reassure them that such fits didn't last long. But Father and Mother were obviously unconvinced. Their strained smiles resembled nothing so much as the facial contortions some people display when in the agony of gastric disturbances. Why hadn't she told me that her parents were active prohibitionists!

When the family asked me to go to church, I told them I preferred to commune with nature; so I took my trusty slingshot and struck out across the vast expanse of wheat stubble. The landscape was alive with blackbirds and meadowlarks. Ah, what a paradise! I thought of Wordsworth and his "host of golden daffodils." Old habits surged to the surface as I remembered perilous climbs in search of birds' nests, and I leveled for the kill. I had lost some skill in wielding the primitive weapon, but before midafternoon I had winged several plump larks who were so young that they hadn't yet learned to avoid immigrant lads drawn by the scent of meat.

When I had plucked, dressed, and singed them, I sauntered toward the farmhouse much excited and a little dubious. When I announced that I intended to cook them for dinner, my hosts were horrified, though they tried desperately to cling to the amenities. The father was clearly annoyed by a foreigner who killed songbirds with undisguised glee. Even my blonde madonna distorted her lovely face in wrinkles of disgust. "You're not *really* going to eat them!" What was I to say? I certainly hadn't slaughtered the plump little fellows for fun. In fact, I had never hunted in all my life just for the sport, as many Americans do. And so as I prepared the larks for the broiler, I tried to convince them that I was not insane. I told them that in Europe the swallow, the thrush, the fig-pecker, and other small fry are accepted as rare delicacies; that many a poor man in Italy has bought his lone pair of boots by providing the rich burgher's table with skewered sparrows. "Oh, I couldn't bear the thought of eating songbirds!"

"The hell you couldn't. The trouble with you is that you have never had to subsist on pilchards and *polenta*. And how about the birds that *don't* sing? What of the lovely duck and the mute grouse? Haven't they as much right to life, liberty, and the pursuit of worms as the noisy bobolink? Besides, if only you would overcome your sentimental nonsense about food, you would find the lark more juicy, delicate, and full of flavor than any fowl you are so ready to kill without batting an eye." That's what I would have said had I been Hotspur.

During dinner I ate the larks, head, bones and all, with more than permissible relish, as I continued to talk what was Greek to them all. I told them that when a farmer in Italy butchers a hog, if he is fortunate enough to own one, he eats everything except the squeal. The less fortunate eat the viscera—lungs, liver, heart, intestines—and sell most of the carcass in order to clothe their children.

They were duly impressed by the account, but I could tell by the expression on their faces that they had cattle on the range, hogs in the sty, and fowl in the hen yard; that they considered my hunt of the larks sheer impertinence. I also realized that the fusion of two cultures in marriage is an undertaking for which neither the blond madonna nor I had the necessary talents. For the remainder of my visit, otherwise very pleasant, I stuck to beef and pork; but when I departed, I knew I had left forever a beautiful maiden and a wheat ranch.

—*The Unprejudiced Palate*

LEAN YEARS, HAPPY YEARS

"THE CURFEW TOLLS the knell of parting day." My work is done. The time is April 1983, the "cruellest month," according to the poet of *The Waste Land*. I have never found it so! And the April of this year is especially dear to me. For I have begun the eightieth year of my life and the seventieth year of my residence in America. And by a happy coincidence, in a few days I shall deliver the manuscript of this, my eighth book, to my editor.

The "cruellest" month? Not so for me! This morning, while the birds were chirping and twittering their epithalamia, and I was humming "Whan that Aprill with his shoures soote..." I pressed the seed for a second row of peas into the fertile soil. The ones in the first row, sown in mid-February, were about to begin their ascent up the supporting poles. Then I fed each of my artichoke plants a handful of urea. How they love that white, crystalline compound, found in mammalian urine! But then— there is no accounting for the vagaries of taste.

My next labor was more muscular, the sort that makes one

sweat, a corrective for prolonged sitting at one's desk. Remember what Emerson said about the therapeutic virtue of such labor. I prepared the soil for sowing pole beans later in the month. I spread manure over the area and incorporated it into the ground by spading. Then I raked the spaded area to achieve a neat, even surface, smoothed the hillocks, removed stones and other rubble. And when all this was done, I mopped my brow, put away my garden tools, and stood for a moment to survey what I had done and to make sure that it was properly done. It was; and I was happy.

I took another look at the artichoke plants. The fruit-bearing stem was beginning to rise from the root crown. How many laterals would it have? Would each bear an artichoke of edible size? Had the roots yet begun to assimilate the urea? I was not impatient, just curious, wanting to know the precise mechanism by which roots ingest such putrid stuff as manure and urea, and transform it into nutrients that give the end products of plants their total character. Despairing that I would never know such secrets of Nature, I simply told the plants to get on with it, so that I might have fried artichoke hearts by the middle of May.

It was midday now and I was hungry. What should I eat? Leeks and chard and witloof chicory and Savoy cabbage had survived the winter. Why not a frittata made with a combination of the first two? Excellent idea! With a muttered farewell to the kitchen garden, I rushed into the house and took a shower. Then I went to the cellar to fetch a bottle of the Holy Blood of the grape, vintage Cabernet, 1971, pressed from perfect grapes sent to me from the Napa Valley. While in the cellar, it being the time to top the barrels, I added a bottle to each of the two sixty-gallon casks and a half bottle to the one of thirty-gallon capacity. With that bit of pleasant cellar work done, I returned to the kitchen, pulled the cork from the bottle, poured myself half a glass and drank it quickly in order to restore to the body the fluid I had lost as sweat; quickly, I say, for in ministering to the needs of the body, there are some things that must not be postponed.

The wine was such that only appropriate metaphors can suggest its total character: authoritative, masculine, imperious, sacramental. It reminded me of what Dante meant when he said of a great wine: "Behold what happens when the heat of the sun transforms the humor that flows in the vine." I knew, when I did my cellar work on the perfect grapes, that the wine would be great; and the promise of greatness was there. But it would take another five years in the bottle to achieve it.

When I had made the frittata, the lost fluid in my body now restored, I, happy as the grass is green, sat down to enjoy my well-earned lunch. The indispensable bread had been baked the day before. Only one thing was lacking to extract from the moment its full measure of joy—my wife. She and I always klink glasses by way of grace when we sit down to dinner. She was at her club assisting in the final arrangements for its annual arts and crafts fair. So before taking the ritual first sip of wine, I held my glass up to her image, winked, brought the glass to my lips, set it down, and attacked the frittata.

Therefore, reconsider the values by which you want to live, grow your own, cook your own, make your own wine. Live in harmony with Nature. And may you find the promised fatness that inheres in the lean and therefore happy years.

—*Lean Years, Happy Years*

GARDEN
AND TABLE

WHY GARDEN?

WHY SHOULD ONE bother to till a cut of the land on which he lives and grow much of what he needs for his daily dinner? The reasons are several, but the most compelling is this: the kitchen garden is an indispensable aid in the attainment of a day-by-day good cuisine. Or put it this way: without a kitchen garden—that plot of land on which one grows herbs, vegetables, and some fruit—it is not possible to produce decent and savory food for the dinner table. This generalization admits no exceptions; it is as sound as the assertion that a stone thrown in the air must return to earth. And since a fine dinner after the day's labor contributes so much to one's well-being, I may state, further, that the kitchen garden is an indispensable aid in the achievement of the Good Life. Are you convinced? Of course! Then you must procure the necessary tools and become a gardener.

In urging this, I assume that you are a normal human being, male or female, young enough to stand on your feet and work with your hands; but most of all I must assume that you are eager to welcome hints on how you can improve your cuisine. And I must also cherish the hope that, should you be rather abstemious, or of that wretched crew who take pride in "eating anything," this little volume may persuade you to join that enlightened company who, as Dr. Johnson put it two hundred years ago, "mind their belly very studiously and very carefully." In other words, I assume that you are one of us; and I therefore urge you with confidence to build yourself a garden and become an expert, happy gardener.

Let us first be clear on what we mean by the word "garden." The dictionary defines it as "a plot of ground devoted to the cultivation of useful or ornamental plants." There is, of course, a distinction between plants that are ornamental and plants that are useful; when I use the word "gardening" my reference is invariably to the cultivation of those plants, such as asparagus, that are used as food; and those, such as rosemary, that are used to make food taste good. In other words, my approach to gardening is fundamentally utilitarian. I cultivate as much of the necessary herbs, vegetables, and fruit as time and place and space will allow, in order to enjoy a fine, even a distinguished, dinner every day.

Fundamentally utilitarian, yes. However, I am not unaware of the aesthetics of gardening. I am easily moved by the beauty in a bed of parsley, a head of cauliflower, a patch of healthy, succulent endive in vigorous growth. Even as the poet's heart leaped up when he beheld a host of golden daffodils, so mine throbs when I behold a row of meticulously cultivated cauliflowers, their compact, snow-white heads set in leafy ruffs of emerald green. So please don't put me down as an insensitive Benthamite. My sense of what is useful does not exclude a sense of what is lovely. I cultivate a garden for its utility, to eat that which I grow, but there is also pleasure in doing it and in beholding the fruit of my labor. When, during the growing season, I go to my garden, as I do nearly every day, and look with pleasure at my bed of parsley, am I moved primarily by its indubitable loveliness? Or is my heart throb occasioned by the thought of how marvelously the minced parsley leaves will enhance the flavor of my omelet? The question is not fair, and I invoke the Fifth. In obedience to my nature I till the soil; I sow and reap the total harvest.

I said that you must build a garden, and "build" is the proper word. Wherever you may live, on whatever plot of land that is your own, you will have to convert a portion of that land into a garden plot. With pick and shovel, rake and hoe and barrow, you may have to dig up a portion of the lawn, level a slope, build retaining walls, wheel out hardpan and rocks and wheel in fine topsoil, or make heavy earth more friable by raking into it sandy soil rich in humus. With tools and with your hands you will give shape to your garden and prepare it to receive the seed. You will build your garden.

There will be joy in the building; there will be joy in contemplating that which you have built; there will be joy in the sowing; there will be joy in following the progress from seed into fruit; there will be joy in the harvest; and there will be the greatest pleasure in eating the fruit of your labor. If you have not known this pleasure, then you have been deprived of much that is good for both the body and the soul! Therefore, decide and act. Don't be a Prufrock wavering in indecision, measuring out your life with a coffee spoon. The shovel is the measure appropriate to a man. Strip to the waist; let the sweat pour down your brow; dig in; put down your roots. And enjoy a manifold harvest.

So, having taken in hand the shovel and the hoe, you have

become a dedicated gardener and a member of an ancient and numerous society. The Great Creator built the first garden and created the prototypes of the complete gardener. Man first appears not in an armory or in a countinghouse but in a garden; and when he had sinned and lost his Eden, he was sent forth to till the ground whence he was taken, and to earn his bread by the sweat of his brow. The Old Testament is so rich in horticultural imagery that one may fairly think of the prophets and psalmists as dedicated gardeners: *They that have gathered the corn shall eat it and praise the Lord; and they that have grown the wine shall drink it in the courts of my holiness....*

A glance at the considerable library of garden literature, and it is at once obvious that some of the wisest and best of mankind have delighted in gardens. Horace had his garden and his orchard; Virgil celebrated agricultural pursuits in his *Georgics*. Shakespeare compared competent kings to complete gardeners and well-ordered commonwealths to well-cultivated gardens; and when his Brutus was troubled and could not sleep, Shakespeare sent him to his garden to ponder his dilemma. John Evelyn, the famous diarist, Robert Walpole, the first Earl of Oxford, William Temple, the seventeenth-century statesman, and Sir Francis Bacon are a few among the many illustrious men who have delighted in gardens. The Baron Bettino Ricasoli, in the middle of the nineteenth century, withdrew from the turbulence of public affairs and settled in Brolio Castle in the Chianti region, where he devoted the rest of his life to agronomy and viticulture. The amiable Londoner Charles Lamb, when he went to live in the country, took pleasure in cultivating a small plot of ground behind his house and "watched with interest the progress toward maturity of his

Windsor pears and jargonelles."

But it was Sir Francis Bacon, that probing, empirical, and far-ranging mind, who, having studied gardening as an experimental science, finally defined its total goodness in these words: "God Almighty first planted a garden; and, indeed, it is the purest of human pleasures; it is the greatest refreshment to the spirits of man; without which buildings and palaces are but gross handy-works; and a man shall ever see that, when ages grow to civility and elegance, man comes to build stately sooner than to garden finely: as if gardening were the greater perfection."

I remember that when I was a child less than ten years of age, old enough to spade and to hoe and to put seed into the ground, I marveled at the miracle of seed into fruit, mine as good and lovely as that from seed put into the ground by older hands than mine. And now, several decades later, I still marvel at the same miracle, and at all the good things I can grow for the table on a patch of ground so tiny that, from its center, the wind with me, I can spit to its every boundary. As I work on that handful of earth and find myself so easily, so ingenuously excited by such a commonplace phenomenon as the growth of the soil, I have the most vivid perception of Bacon's meaning when he said of gardening that it is the purest of human pleasures and the greatest refreshment to the spirit. More than once when the well was dry and the mood of Ecclesiastes threatened, I followed Brutus to the garden, where all was sweet fruitfulness and nothing was in vain. And I have often wondered, walking among my growing family of vegetables, whether Lord Bacon and Baron Ricasoli and all the great men who delighted in gardening marveled even as I did as a child, and still do as a man, at the recurring miracle of seed into flower. Is there not something that is just right, simply and sweetly good in tilling the soil, sowing the seed, reaping the harvest?

But let us return to something more tangible. Andrew Borde, physician to his "prepotent Majeste" King Henry VIII, another British gentleman who minded his belly very studiously and very carefully, went on record with this practical observation: "It is a commodious and pleasant thing to a mansion to have an orchard of sundry fruits; but it is more commodious to have a fair garden, replete with herbs of aromatic and redolent savour."

Fair, commodious, pleasant! Utility and ornament! Consider, for a moment, the garden as a "commodious" adjunct to one's "mansion"; note what it means in terms of simple well-being, convenience, and domestic economy. Let us suppose that we are gardeners. We have pork cutlets in the cooler. The dinner hour is nigh and we are hungry. Hunger in a garden has a way of relating to the garden. How shall we enhance the cutlets? We go to the fair garden, replete with herbs of aromatic and redolent savor. We take of these what we want for an appropriate herb marinade. We lave the cutlets with it, sprinkle them with salt and pepper, and put them in the broiler. We pull the cork on a bottle of red wine and as we sip, the aroma of the the broiling cutlets in our nostrils, we count our blessings. Then we sit to supper and know the meaning of simple well-being!

But there is yet more of well-being, much more! During the growing season, the garden is a continuous source of fresh vegetables. Now what, precisely, is a fresh vegetable? Anyone who is in the least aware of what he buys at the supermarket must have been many times disappointed when he searched the vegetable bins: the lettuce was wilted; the carrots looked old and tired; the green beans had the pox. With a shrug of futility he took what was least offensive and hoped for better luck next time. The advantage enjoyed by the gardener is that he is never disappointed; his carrots are always taken directly from the garden to the kitchen. And so are the green beans, taken from the vine *when they are prime for the table and cooked immediately*. A vegetable is not necessarily fresh because it is brought immediately from the garden to the kitchen; it may have lost its freshness before it was harvested. A vegetable is completely fresh when it is taken in its prime and brought directly from the garden to the kitchen.

Note now the meaning of Andrew Borde's "commodious" in terms of the practical convenience that a garden provides. When well planned, executed, and maintained, the garden will have in it such basic herbs and vegetables as can be grown in a given region, and these will be at hand throughout the growing season. That in itself is the great convenience: to have in one's own garden whatever vegetables one wants, and to have them at the moment he wants them. But the garden is a convenience in other less spectacular, but no less important, ways. A cook needs a sprig of parsley to execute a recipe. Three steps into the garden and he has it. Or he may need a bay leaf, a leaf of chard, a few leaf ends of celery, a small carrot, to flavor a beef broth. Lacking a garden he would have to buy these ingredients in quantities considerably greater than his need, since vegetables are now sold in bunches or packaged in cellophane. What a convenience, then, to take them fresh from the garden in exactly the amount needed. And, incidentally, what a savings! Or, again, the need for a certain indispensable ingredient may be discovered at the last minute, when kettles are boiling and skillets are simmering. The lamb stew is assembled and cooking. All it wants to round out the flavor is a bit of fresh, minced rosemary. And there is the herb, a few paces from the kitchen door. Very commodious indeed!

Granted, one may say; but does it pay? The economy of a kitchen garden is often questioned by people who have little knowledge of what produce costs and no idea how much can be grown on a small plot of land. Typical of such is a man in our neighborhood I call Uncle Harry for no better reason than that he looks as if he might be Uncle Harry to the world. He is a realtor who owns much land hereabout and walks around a great deal, stopping by property he owns and by land he would like to own and wondering all the while which of the many deals he has plotted is ready for execution. He is a fattish, hearty man of affairs who habitually thinks big. He passed by one day while I was setting out cabbage plants. "What the hell are you doing on this fine day?" he asked. And when I told him he said, "Hell, it don't pay. For a couple of bucks you can buy enough cabbage to fatten a steer. Seed, fertilizer, water, labor—you add all these up and you're losing dough. Get wise. Go play golf." I told him I thought he was right, and that made him very happy. "Hell, yes," he said. "It don't pay."

But Uncle Harry was completely wrong, even about fattening a steer on cabbage. A small kitchen garden, properly managed, will put money in your purse. Keep it in production as long as the weather in your region permits; exploit fully the resources of your land; do all that needs to be done, properly and at the right time; and you will prove Uncle Harry wrong.

—*The Food Lover's Garden*

HERBS

To SAY THAT herbs are the soul of cookery is to affirm, metaphorically, a culinary truth: their judicious and imaginative use in the kitchen results in a distinguished, sophisticated cuisine. Don't be discouraged by the words "distinguished" and "sophisticated"; such a cuisine is easily within your competence. Submit yourself to a very simple test: roast half a chicken with herbs and roast the other half without them. Now smell and taste the two parts. You smile with approval! You glow with culinary confidence! The seasoned part smells and tastes better than the other! Your cuisine is now distinguished and sophisticated. And wasn't it all very simple ? The judicious and imaginative use of herbs did the trick. Voilà!

Is it any wonder, then, that in Europe and the Orient, where the use of herbs in cooking is as common as the use of salt and pepper, there should be a mythology of herbs, a veritable herb lore, just as there is a mythology, a lore of wine? It is, indeed, so extensive and so diverse, ranging from the romantic to the pathological, that it would require volumes to anthologize the best of it. Much of the lore, particularly the anecdotal material accepted as knowledge, has its genesis more in desire than in experience: rosemary leaves strewn under the bed will prevent bad dreams; munching caraway seeds will bring a bloom to the cheeks of pale-faced maidens; garlic juice in the nostrils is a safeguard against the plague; a sprig of anise tied to the bed-post will make one look young in the morning; an indifferent face may be made fair by washing it with an infusion of white wine and rosemary leaves. There is, of course, no proof for these quaint and interesting claims. Wine is a good and pleasant thing, and sweet basil will do wonders to fettuccine. From these facts it is an easy leap to the wish-conclusion that herbs and wine are rich in miraculous virtues. Nor is such wishful thinking regret-table. There is, in fact, much good in it, for it affirms in many delightful ways that wine and herbs relate very closely to the aesthetic in man's nature, his desire for that which is pleasant.

And that which is pleasant, all that contributes to purely sensuous pleasures, all that urges one to abandon Calvin and fol-low Epicurus and seek a measure of redemption in joyous liv-ing has been for too long suspect in an America that was forged in the Puritan ethic. The Anglo-Saxons owe their culinary her-itage of mashed potatoes and somber gravy to the teachers and preachers, statesmen and philosophers whose *busyness* and aus-terity fashioned that essentially gloomy and stern view of life. A dish that smelled good and tasted even better than it smelled, and so was eaten with fresh appetite and heightened pleasure, would certainly stimulate appetites of another sort and urge one on to pleasures more visceral, especially if the savory food were accom-panied by a glass of wine. And that would spell damnation. So boil the potatoes and water the roast, and fill the dinner goblets with water, and let each one rejoice in the austere pursuit of business.

It was a cruel philosophy rooted in the Middle Ages and supported by a misreading of the Sacred Book. It attempted to legislate out of existence certain wholesome appetites of the flesh, man's instinctive search for those experiences that yield immediate pleasure, and, in the long pull, it failed. Prohibition is out; gourmet cooking and wine are in. In the America of today the view of life fostered by the Puritan ethic has been purged of much of its sobriety. Many, many Americans have made the happy discovery that there is neither sin nor wickedness in a sprig of rosemary and a glass of wine; that, other things being equal, a sophisticated cuisine, by increasing total contentment, is more likely to promote the good than the bad life. And this sane trend in America's coming of age is attested by the growing interest in a sophisticated cuisine, in wine as the indispensable dinner beverage, and in herbs as "the very soul of good cookery." I owe the phrase to Marcellina, about whom I shall have something to say later.

Culinary herbs! the lovely aromatics! The secret of good cookery is in the use of these. And since they are not generally available at the supermarket, you must grow them yourself. For the dry herbs, in the very process of drying, lose their spicy essence; at best, they are only an inadequate substitute for the fresh. I shall tell you more about them, how the best of them may be grown and used, but first, a word about my own interest in herbs. The intent here is to dramatize as vividly as I can the statement that fresh herbs, the lovely aromatics, are indeed the soul of cookery.

It is my good fortune that I was born in Italy, of peasant

parents who were both good cooks, and in a culture where the pleasures of the table were applauded even by the clergy. How well I remember the corpulent, rosy-cheeked parish priest sitting at our table and drinking a toast to Mother's savory broth! A dish of good food, whether it was a soup, a stew, a vegetable, a fish, was the preoccupation of everyone. They openly exulted in it, talked about it, named the flavoring agent that gave it character, or suggested how it might have been improved with a little less x and a bit more y. When they sat together in the evening knitting or mending, housewives talked frequently about cookery, wondering with what herbs and condiment they might contrive a good dish out of the lowly raw materials they had to work with. They sometimes disagreed on what herbs and spices should be used to flavor a dish of frogs, for example, and then there would be a spirited discussion in which even the men and older children participated. Everyone was interested in eating well, and no one even faintly suspected that delicious food would nudge one toward damnation.

In such an environment I passed my early childhood. Then we emigrated to America, where, with an abundance of good raw materials at their disposal, my parents—Father usually cooked on Sundays—achieved a very fine cuisine. Every dinner was in some way distinguished, and its "secret," known to every French and Italian housewife, was the use of fresh herbs.

Since I was very young and very busy with the myriad interests of the young, I took my culinary good fortune pretty much for granted. Until I went away to college. Then I realized that when I had moved from our home in the country and gone to Seattle I had left behind a very fine cuisine the like of which

I could not find in the university community. And no wonder! The entire state, the whole Northwest, had not yet discovered garlic! But I *must* find it, I told myself. I *must* have an occasional dinner such as I had enjoyed at home.

And find it I did in the homes of Italian immigrants in Seattle's "Little Italy." Even before I had finished with registration, I began my exploration of the Italian community, intent on cultivating the friendship of some of the then youngish housewives who were reputed to be good cooks. Within a year I was on "family" terms with more than a dozen good cooks. Some were from the north of Italy; some from the central provinces; two were from the south. They all had large kitchen gardens in which they grew their herbs and vegetables. Excited by the abundance they had found in America, they were all intent on perfecting their cuisine. They consulted with one another, exchanged ideas, and sometimes resolutely disagreed on whether a certain herb was essential in preparing a dish.

Since I was frequently in the home of one or the other of them when they visited in the evening after dinner, I learned a great deal from them about cookery and the use of herbs. Occasionally I was on hand while one of them was preparing dinner; then I would observe and ask questions. And when I went home I would tell Mother about some of the dishes I had eaten and liked; she, delighted with my interest in cookery, would tell me how she prepared the same dish. In this way I learned that the secret of a fine cuisine was the use of fresh herbs and that without them, food could be made good enough to eat, but never good enough to inspire praise.

The two best cooks I met in Seattle's "Little Italy" happened

to be neighbors. Let me simply call them Angelina and Marcellina. They were also good gardeners. I was fascinated by these
two women because in addition to being good cooks, they were
strikingly different in character and bound to each other by a
subtle, silent culinary competition. Each was certain that she was
the better of the two, and when they talked about cookery, the
intent was somehow to get this point across without seeming to
do anything of the sort. Of that good-humored competition I
was the happy beneficiary, for when one learned that the other
had made fettuccine for me, she promptly invited me to dinner
and gave me fettuccine made her way. "Are they good?" she would
ask as she watched me eat them with my customary groaning sort
of relish. And without waiting for a reply she would add, with
the subtlest touch of irony, "Of course, Marcellina [Angelina]
makes them better." With a wink, a gesture, an ambiguous raising
of the brows, but without speaking a word, I had to praise the one
without seeming to betray the other.

Angelina was from Tuscany, the land of Italy's finest olive
oil; Marcellina was from Parma, the land of butter and cheese.
The one used olive oil exclusively in her cookery; the other used
much butter. And they often argued about which was the
better fat for cooking. Marcellina dressed her fettuccine with
butter, cheese, and fresh basil, an herb for which she had a special affection. When it was in season she often carried a sprig of
it with her for sniffing when she went visiting. Angelina insisted that the best dressing for fettuccine was the classic meat sauce
used for spaghetti. In preparing a roasting chicken for the oven,
Marcellina insisted that Angelina was wrong in adding celery
leaves to certain other herbs. And so they argued, and each

looked to me for support of her views. I ate heartily the proof of their theories and somehow managed to keep them both happy and cooking for me.

It was in listening to their talk about cookery that I became aware, for the first time, that in speaking of herbs the Italian housewives generally used the word *odorini*. It is the endearing plural diminutive of the Italian word *odore*, "odor." Thus, *odorini* may be literally translated as the "dear little odors or fragrances." Angelina and Marcellina, chatting about culinary herbs, revealed their affectionate regard for them by using the term. "Lovely aromatics" is a fairly good translation, and there is no doubt that they are the soul of cookery. On this point, Angelina and Marcellina were in complete agreement.

—*The Food Lover's Garden*

EDUCATING
THE SENSES

Do you have an olfactory or taste memory? Can you recall an odor in its absence? Let us say that a year or so ago you sampled a wine with a distinct odor and taste. Could you now identify that wine among several others submitted to you, as certain wine connoisseurs can allegedly do? The potential for such a memory is there for anyone with unimpaired organs of odor and taste; but it must be cultivated and improved, as it has been in professional sniffers and tasters.

Impairment of sight and hearing, whether caused by old age or a defect in the very young, can be corrected by hearing aids and eyeglasses. Organs of taste, smell, and touch, however, do not degenerate with age in anyone who reaches the golden decades sound of body and mind. Assiduously cultivated, the sensitivity of these organs can even be improved as one grows older. And this is a blessing: an octogenarian who cannot recapture the joy of a brisk run against the spring wind may yet smell a rose, feel the warmth of a dear one's hand, or fully enjoy the pleasures of the dinner table.

What is required to improve the sensitivity of the organs of smell, taste, and touch is conscious exercise. Conscious, I say, for one may go through life smelling, tasting, and touching without being particularly aware of the inherent pleasure. Consider, for example, a chicken that has been stuffed with rosemary, parsley, celery, onion, and garlic, and laved with olive oil, roasting in the oven. The fragrance permeates the room. Someone with a cultivated sense of smell enters the room and immediately reacts: eyes close for concentration, lips press together, brows wrinkle, the olfactory organ sniffs knowingly. He or she may not be able to identify it, but what matters is an awareness, and enjoyment, of the fragrance.

To press the inquiry further, would the kitchen visitor, having smelled and tasted the roasted chicken, recall its smell and taste some time later? Most certainly, if the person had purposively and continuously exercised the organs of smell and taste, and then made an additional effort to remember aromas and flavors.

In some individuals, certain odors and tastes are fixed in the memory without a conscious effort. When I was a young boy in Italy, we lived near a swamp where frogs were abundant. We cooked them frequently in a tomato sauce in which the principal flavoring agent was *puleggio*. I was especially fond of the sauce. Its fragrance haunted me after we settled in America in a region where there were no frogs. It occurred to me when I grew up that I might try to cook fish in the same sauce. But where in Seattle, sixty years ago, was there a greengrocer who had puleggio? Nor could I find it in the kitchen gardens of the Italian immigrants I knew in "Garlic Gulch." They had never even heard of it.

Thirty years later, I found my puleggio. It was in San Francisco's North Beach, in a settlement more Italian than any community in Italy. I was shopping in Lippi's market, and, always interested in vegetables, I explored the produce section. There were cardoons, small artichokes, sweet fennel, various kinds of chicory, and an herb bouquet that *looked* familiar. I pressed a leaf between my thumb and index finger. One sniff and I leaped for joy, to Signor Lippi's astonishment. "What have you found?" he wanted to know. "Puleggio!"

He wrapped a small bunch in moist paper and I took it home. The few branches I placed in water in a glass on the windowsill developed roots, which I planted in the garden. I now find seedlings in several places among the vegetables. Its botanical name, I have learned, is *Mentha pulegium*.

So now I can reproduce the sauce whose fragrance was long ago fixed in my memory. It may not be precisely as my mother made it, and, lacking frogs, I use it in cooking fish. Here is my method: Dust lightly with flour a fish fillet or steak. Brown it on both sides in olive oil and butter. Remove it onto a dish. In the same skillet, sauté a mince of shallots and garlic until they are transparent, using low heat to avoid scorching. Add to this a heaping tablespoon of parsley and *Mentha pulegium* minced together, and what salt and pepper you wish. Sprinkle over the whole a bit of arrowroot for thickening, and stir with a spatula. To half a cup of stock add a dash of Tabasco, the juice of half a lemon, a jigger of dry vermouth, and a teaspoon of tomato sauce. Pour over the sautéed ingredients and simmer over low heat until the sauce is dense but fluid. Return the fish to the skillet, spoon the sauce over it, give the pan a professional shake, simmer for a few minutes—and 'tis done.

Having done this and achieved a certain transcendence in gastronomy, why not, in gratitude, pull the cork from a bottle of Robert Mondavi Chardonnay Reserve? Sniff it carefully and try to remember the smell. It is very close to the great Montrachet, the white Burgundy of France. And thereafter, you will know an authentic chardonnay when you smell and taste one.

Biologists tell us that in humans, as in animals, the act of smelling is very much like the act of thinking: both are functions of the appropriate brain cells. Yet while our brains are functionally much greater than those of animals, our sense of smell is much less acute than many of theirs. Compared with such animals as dogs, wolves, and rats in olfactory sensitivity, man is, as Lewis Thomas writes, "a biological failure." And because of this deficiency, we may never know "how much of the world we are missing." Apparently we have much to learn about the biology of odor. "We may fairly gauge the future of biological science, centuries ahead," Thomas says, "by estimating the time it will take to reach a complete, comprehensive understanding of odor." Meanwhile, we have every reason to believe that we may each lessen the amount of the world we are missing by cultivating the sensitivity of our sense organs.

—*Seattle Weekly*

SOFFRITTO

THE FRENCH USE a *bouquet garni*, a combination of herbs tied together as a flavoring agent and removed when its flavor has been imparted to the sauce or stew. The Italian cook uses a *soffritto*. (The word is the past participle of *soffriggere*, to sauté lightly.) It is a mince of a combination of herbs, usually with some salt pork. When these are sautéed, the soffritto is incorporated into whatever dish requires it. Thus, a soffritto of onion, garlic, parsley, celery leaves, mushrooms, sage, rosemary, and salt pork, with the addition of a small tin of tomato sauce, is an excellent sauce for pasta.

There are many culinary herbs that may be used in making a soffritto, as well as in other ways. Since the ones I have had in my own garden for forty years will do as well for you as they have for me, let me tell you about them and some of the ways in which they may be used to good advantage in day-by-day cookery. If you want to know more, I suggest that you procure a monograph on the entire herb family.

The indispensable core of the herbs I grow and use almost daily is a group of perennials: rosemary, sage, thyme, English pennyroyal (*Mentha pulegium*), and tarragon. The first three are evergreen in our mild climate, and in the spring, they achieve a certain luxuriance of new growth. I have plants of each growing in various parts of the garden so that if one dies, the loss will not be total. Tarragon renews itself yearly from the root crown. In such a mild winter as the last, pennyroyal remains green enough for use, though it also renews itself from seeds dropped by the mature plant in early autumn. Thus, for these many years, I have never been without this group of herbs. When the winter has been severe, I have protected them by mulching the roots and covering the plant.

Rosemary is used in flavoring lamb as well as in various sauces. A few sprigs of it and three or four cloves of garlic will spell transcendence in oven-roasted potatoes. Put some olive oil in a shallow roasting pan—enough to drench the bottom. Put it in a 400-degree oven. When smoking hot, add quartered, peeled potatoes and give the pan a vigorous shaking to coat the potatoes with the hot oil. Shake the pan once more when they begin to brown, and add the coarsely chopped garlic and rosemary, and salt and pepper to taste. When the potatoes are a golden color, remove them with a slotted spoon onto absorbent paper and proceed with the eating thereof, being careful not to burn your eager palate. Then whisper, "Potato, thou art transcended!"

Both rosemary and sage—with garlic and onion—may be used in roasting, frying, and sautéing veal, pork, and poultry. Other ways in which they may be used, I shall leave to your imagination. Experimenting is the name of the culinary game. Do so with all the herbs. Use tarragon and pennyroyal as the dominating flavoring agents in cooking fish. Try a chicken sautéed with tarragon, or use it in flavoring vinegar: a cup of its leaves to a quart of vinegar; let the infusion stand for a week or so, and you will have enough to flavor a gallon of vinegar. Use thyme in stews and in baked beans.

The herbs I grow yearly from seed, no less indispensable than the above, are basil, chervil, and parsley. The first of these is strictly a hot-weather annual, so I wait until the warming trend is permanent, in late May, before I sow the seed. The other two, sown weeks ago, have already germinated, but it is not too late to sow their seeds now. Parsley is so hardy, with its long, tough taproot, that it easily survives a reasonably mild winter. I am now using what was sown last spring while the plant completes its life cycle. By the time the seed-bearing stem is fully grown and its leaves diminish and wither, the new crop will be ready for use.

Thank Nature and the Pacific Northwest for that, for Pellegrini without parsley—good gracious! I am reminded of what my bibulous grandmother used to say: "A dinner without wine is like a kiss from a man without a mustache." Fortunately for my peace of mind, when I first heard her say that, I was too young to catch its tragic implications.

To the above herbs, I would add carrot, chard, leek, bay leaf, onion, and garlic, for flavoring agents in making stock and soups, and in other soffrittos.

I have given you points of departure. The rest is in your capable hands, instructed by your culinary imagination and driven by an indomitable will to mind your belly very carefully and very studiously.

—*Seattle Weekly*

LAMB

OF ALL THE animal flesh, furred or feathered, eaten by man, not alone for nourishment but also for purely gustatory reasons, lamb deserves to be placed at the head of the list. Even in beef-eating England, Isabella Beeton, whose *Book of Household Management*, published in 1861, enjoyed almost scriptural authority in the English-speaking world for half a century, wrote that lamb was of all wild or domesticated animals, without exception, the most useful to man as food. We have this bit of information on the authority of Waverly Root, in his excellent book titled *Food*. The people of the Mediterranean Basin and the Middle East would agree with this judgment. And others ought to.

And to this I would add that we have scriptural authority for celebrating lamb, both for what the wooly creature is in itself, for its "personality," and for its flesh as distinctly gourmet food. Recall *Agnus Dei*, the Lamb of God, which derives from John 1:29, "Behold the Lamb of God, which taketh away the sin of the world," and from Isaiah 53:7, "He is brought as a lamb to the slaughter, and as a sheep before her shearers is dumb, so he openeth not his mouth." And Alexander Pope to the same effect:

The lamb thy luxury, dooms to bleed today,
Had he thy reason, would he skip and play?
Pleased to the last, he crops the flowery food,
And licks the hand just raised to shed his blood.

Men of letters, gastronomes as a class, have mentioned animal flesh as food. Charles Lamb wrote a dissertation on roast pig;
and Byron remembered the *beccafico* in one of his poems. The
name means fig-pecker, a songbird that pecks figs and is considered a delicacy in Italy. But it was William Blake who wrote a
classic lyric on lamb:

Little Lamb, who made thee?
Dost thou know who made thee?
Little Lamb, I'll tell thee:
He is called by thy name,
For he calls himself a Lamb.
He is meek and he is mild;
He became a little child.
I a child and thou a lamb,
We are called by his name.
Little Lamb, God bless thee!
Little Lamb, God bless thee!

Such is the scriptural authority for the emergence of lamb
as the appropriate animal flesh to be eaten in celebration of the
Passover and the Resurrection. Hence, also its name "paschal

lamb," from the Latin *paschalis*, Passover, and the Italian *Pasqua*, Easter.

Proceeding from the clerical to the secular, and strictly on its own merits as animal flesh of unexcelled gustatory virtues, spring lamb as the occasional dinner fare of the highest quality throughout the year has the sanction of all people who, in the words of Doctor Johnson, mind their belly very studiously and very carefully. Since I belong in that category by family tradition and my own insistence on the finest dinner daily—and what requirement is more praiseworthy in this blessed land of abundance?—may I suggest some ways of preparing lamb for the table?

Whether the flesh of lamb is roasted or pan-fried in the skillet or made into a stew, the preferred flavoring agents, in addition to salt and pepper, are garlic, fresh rosemary, capers, parsley, lemon juice, olive oil, and dry vermouth. For a leg of lamb roast proceed thus: Remove the bone. In the resulting cavity, spread two tablespoons of the following all coarsely minced together: three cloves of garlic, a dozen capers, leaves of parsley and rosemary. Salt and pepper. Sprinkle over the whole a tablespoon of olive oil, the juice of half a lemon. Add a sacramental spray of dry vermouth. Enfold the bone in the cavity, tie the whole securely with heavy twine. Roast it medium-rare in a 350-degree oven in a pan just large enough to contain it. Baste occasionally with its own juices enriched with a bit of vermouth.

You are not likely to find this recipe in any of the cookbooks. Nor the following, but have faith in Pellegrini: Place lamb shanks or ribs in an iron skillet in the oven preheated to 375 degrees. When about half done, drain out all the fat. Sprinkle with olive oil; add coarsely cut garlic, a few sprigs of rosemary, a squirt or two of lemon juice fired with a squirt of Tabasco. Salt and pepper to taste. Give the skillet a thoroughly professional shake, return it to the oven, and reduce the heat to 300. In a few minutes, just long enough for them to assimilate the flavoring agents, the ribs will be done. The shanks will require more time. When you eat them, repeat this ritual: Little lambkins, dost thou know who made thee? No? WHY, I MADE THEE!

For lamb chops and steak: Mince finely garlic and rosemary. Put in a small bowl, add olive oil and lemon juice. Remove what fat you can from the chops, rub them with this mixture, salt and pepper to taste, and cook them in a skillet rubbed with butter. When about done, spray them lightly with vermouth.

For a fricassee or stew, cut neck bones and meat from the shoulder in small pieces. Dust them with flour flavored with salt, pepper, and curry powder. Using a heavy skillet, brown them in olive oil. Remove them with a slotted spoon onto a dish. In the same skillet, with no additional fat, sauté onion, celery, carrot, potato, all coarsely chopped and in what quantity desired. To a cup of stock add a squirt of Tabasco, the juice of half a lemon, two tablespoons of tomato sauce, a scant teaspoon of arrowroot for thickening. Stir well and pour over the sauté. The resulting sauce should be dense but fluid. If too dense, add some vermouth. If too fluid, add more arrowroot. Return the meat to the skillet, mix thoroughly, clamp on the lid, and simmer over low heat for five or so minutes.

By way of grace, and remembering the scriptural authority for dining on lamb, vary the ritual thus: Little Lamb, God bless thee for meekly submitting to the slaughter, so that we of the Human Family may nourish our body and indulge our palate with thy flesh, of all the animals the "most useful to man as food."

There are ways of preparing lamb for the table other than those given above. I have given you what you are not likely to find in the cookbooks.

—*Seattle Weekly*

DANDELION

SOME SIXTY YEARS ago, in a class taught by Joseph B. Harrison, one of the great teachers in the liberal arts school of the University of Washington, I read an essay on food, the title and author of which I have forgotten; but there were three imperious commands in it that I will always remember. These were: "Waiter, more bread"; "Waiter, more cheese"; "Waiter, more celery." The author noted, also, that when the waiter put the celery on with the cheese, he knew that we were in the season of mists and mellow fruitfulness, for celery is the harbinger of autumn.

Thus I learned that the happy diner was fond of bread and cheese, and that cheese and celery are complementary edibles. It had been a few years since I had left Italy, where I had frequently lunched on bread and a small wedge of cheese; what was new to me in the prandial equation was the assertion that celery and cheese go together. Figs and prosciutto, yes; bread and cheese, yes. That bread and cheese are a unity in the culinary culture of Italy is reflected in the aphorism *Quei due sono come pane e formaggio*: the given two are as inseparable as bread and cheese.

I recall all this now while I am thinking of another season and its edible harbinger, soon to be brought to the table to complement grilled pork cutlets. The season is spring and its harbinger is dandelion. The name derives from the medieval Latin *dens leonis* and the Middle English *dent de lion*, lion's tooth, so called because of its sharply indented or serrated leaves.

Dandelion and its near relative, chicory, belong to a large family of herbaceous, seed-bearing plants known as Compositae. The one was introduced from Eurasia, the other from Europe. Both are hardy perennials used mostly for the finest of salads in France and Italy. They grow as weeds in meadows, pastures, and other grassy areas. Dandelion bears a low-growing yellow flower, chicory a blue flower on a many-branched stem several feet high. The leaves of both are very much alike in taste and structure.

Of chicory, *Chicorium intybus*, there are many varieties cultivated in France, Belgium, and northern Italy. Since they are hardy and perennial, they easily survive severe winters. The long, tough taproot responds immediately after the thaw, bearing a small, compact rosette of succulent leaves with an incipient stem at its center. When the leaves are about three or so inches long, the rosette is ready for the salad bowl. This occurs at exactly the time the root of the dandelion produces its spring growth. These two harbingers of spring are normally available to me in my kitchen garden toward the end of February.

When I said that such a salad complements grilled pork cutlets, I was speaking generically, for it complements, as well, all flesh and fowl that is grilled, roasted, or pan-fried. In our home we have the season's first dandelion salad with roast pork or cutlets grilled; and we have it on Washington's Birthday. By removing a weed from the land to which I came in search of bread, and contributing ever so slightly to the welfare of the farmer who earns his bread raising hogs and corn, we feel it is a most appropriate way to celebrate the birth of the man who delivered the colonies from the tyranny of George III.

A concluding note: The season for the spring growth of dandelion and chicory is short—three or four weeks. Beyond that the leaves grow apace and become too tough and bitter. For the dressing, use one-third part wine vinegar to two-thirds part olive oil. Add a pinch of curry powder and two cloves of garlic finely minced. If you have it on hand, crumble a bit of blue cheese in it, and perhaps a couple of minced fillets of anchovies. A salad of such greens requires a substantial condiment. If you are serving a fine wine, use lemon juice in the dressing instead of vinegar.

—*Seattle Weekly*

ARTICHOKE

WE LIVE IN an environment that is congenial to the growth of some of the most desirable and expensive members of the vegetable kingdom: Belgian endive, shallots, garlic, and artichokes. The current price of each of the first three is about five dollars a pound, and prime artichokes are now selling for close to a dollar each. If you have a bit of land, the cultivation of these will be richly rewarding in pleasure and dollars. In this column, I shall give you the necessary data on the artichoke: its origin, propagation, cultivation, and modes of preparation for the table.

Known as the globe artichoke, it was first cultivated in southern Italy, then spread to other areas in the Mediterranean basin. It was brought to the United States early in the nineteenth century and is now extensively grown in the central coast counties of California. The plant, *Cynara scolymus*, is an herbaceous perennial of thistle ancestry which thrives in a climate where the summers are sunny, but cool and moist, and the winters are mild. Where the temperature falls to twenty-eight degrees, the growth above ground will be destroyed; but the unaffected root system, deep and woody, will produce new shoots in the spring. If, however, the temperature falls to the low twenties or below, the entire plant will be killed, a loss that can be avoided by such protective measures as mulching and covering with black plastic. In forty years experience with this delectable vegetable, I have lost all my plants only once, years ago in November when the temperature dropped to twelve degrees.

To cultivate the plant properly and use its produce to best advantage in the kitchen, it is well to know its morphology. A mature root crown, three or more years old, will produce several seasonal shoots, in the spring and the fall. These will grow to a height of three feet and a round spread of four or five. The fruit-bearing stem, an inch or more in diameter, rises from the center of the leaf cluster, bearing the developing artichoke at its tip end. As the stem elongates, it produces several lateral branches, each with fruit somewhat smaller than the one on the parent stem. Thus a single shoot from the root crown will produce at least four artichokes. When these have been harvested, the bearing stem is cut at ground level. Soon thereafter, new shoots will rise from the root crown, and one or more will bear fruit. Since the plant is perennial, this fruiting process goes on indefinitely twice a year, in midspring and late fall.

Their marketable portion, the so-called bud, is actually the immature flower head, composed of numerous closely overlaid bracts or scales. The edible portion consists of the tender bases of the bracts, the young flowers, and the receptacle or fleshy base on which the flowers are borne. If the bud, the artichoke, is not removed, it will develop into a purple-centered, thistlelike flower with a head six to eight inches in diameter. At the base of the flower, in the receptacle, will be hundreds of seeds, about the size and shape of sunflower seeds. The artichoke is best for the table when it is about the size of a large lemon and its bracts are tightly closed at the top. As they open and spread, the plant's energy goes to the production of the replicating seeds and the bud becomes tough, bitter, and less edible. The so-called "jumbo" artichoke, with its bracts opening at the top, and its receptacle a mass of developing seeds, has little else to recommend it but its size.

The plant requires loose, well-drained soil to a depth of eighteen or more inches. Propagation is by root section or by a rooted shoot taken from an established plant. Propagated by seed, the plant tends to revert to its thistle ancestry. For continuous quality production, it is well to renew the plant every five or six years. Take up the entire root crown, divide it, and replant the best sections. This may be done after the spring or fall harvest.

The plant requires a fertilizer rich in the urea found in all mammals, such as barnyard manure or "night soil"—human excrement—which is used widely in the Orient and elsewhere. The commercial product is a white crystalline or powdery compound sold in seed stores. A handful applied to the plant early in the spring will yield luxuriant growth and prime buds.

To prepare the artichoke for cooking, cut off the thorny tip end (about half an inch) using a very sharp knife since the bracts are tough. Then cut away the upper part of the outer bracts to the inner ones that are tender and edible. When this is properly done, you will have a pared artichoke, the whole of which is edible, including an inch or so of the stem. Cut in halves or quarters longitudinally, and cook it in one of the following ways.

Boiled in a small quantity of salted water until tender but

firm, artichokes may be served with hollandaise sauce or a sauce
of olive oil, lemon juice, a dash of Tabasco, salt, and pepper. Or
the halves can be sautéed in olive oil, butter, a dash of lemon
juice, garlic, and parsley, then combined with sautéed chicken
for an elegant main course. Combined here means stirred in with
the chicken during its final minutes of cooking. For fried artichokes, cut the halves into three or four slices lengthwise, dredge
in a light batter of egg and flour, and lightly brown on both sides
in enough olive or other oil to cover the bottom of a nonstick
skillet. Drain them on absorbent paper, sprinkle with salt, pepper, and lemon juice, and they will elicit the praise of whoever
eats them.

—*Seattle Weekly*

RABBIT
AND POLENTA

L AST OCTOBER AFTER a mushroom hunt, unable to find
my way out of the forest, I spent a miserable night in the foothills
of the Cascades. As I stated in my column on that frightening
experience, I had gone astray because of the insatiable greed of
my breed of mushroom hunters. Since such a hunter may be a
gentleman in the parlor but eccentric and wicked in his mushroom domain, I shall sketch his profile so that you may avoid a
confrontation with him in the hills.

He is on the hunt at the crack of dawn. He wears his shirt
inside out, carries his quarry in a smelly ancestral pillowcase, and
is armed with a long, sharply pointed rod of steel or hardwood.
He has sworn an oath to keep poachers out of his mushroom
patches and to poach on patches of other hunters. When mushrooms are the prize, especially the species known as *Boletus edulis*,
the scope of all his greed is narrowed to these two goals. Though
in all else he may be as saintly as St. Francis, in the pursuit of these
ends he is more satanic than Satan. He will betray his nearest and
dearest without the slightest twitch of flesh or spirit. He is self-

righteously amoral. His, and only his, is the unalienable right to the entire kingdom of fungi. He especially vents his hatred on amateur mycologists, for when they have found a mushroom area, they lead others to it.

I happen to know the Master of our breed, an Italian, whose nose and eyes were trained from infancy for the hunt. For years I tried in vain to persuade him to take me with him to what he called the Sacred Grove. Finally, after I had made him high on wine, and in exchange for some rare vintages delivered yearly during the mushroom season, he agreed, swore me to secrecy, and made me a member of the satanic breed. On our first hunt together, with his bloodhound nose, he smelled a poacher. "He's here," he said, "a lousy mycologist. I can smell him." He sniffed savagely with that nose grown to enormous size with sniffing. All I could smell was the fragrance of conifers. And soon thereafter, his lynx eyes saw what I could not see—a poacher crouched in the distance.

"Look," he said, pointing with his deadly rod and moving toward him through the dense undergrowth with the ease of a cougar stalking its prey. "Follow me and learn how to deal with poachers." I did; but before I could see the villain, the Master stopped. He lit a cigarette, inhaled deeply, exhaled, removed his hat, mopped his brow with the back of his hand, and muttered fiercely, "The bastard saw me and fled." Then he vented his fury with such a flow of obscenities in Italian that I dare not translate it. Thus relieved, he snuffed out the cigarette, lit another, took a couple of drags on it, twirled it reflectively with thumb and index finger, and pronounced a mournful soliloquy in the colloquial Italian of Tuscan hill towns. Turned into more or less respectable free verse, this was its substance:

I hate him for he is a poaching mycologist,
But more for that in base simplicity,
He blabs about the Sacred Grove
Where mushrooms thrive: the fat boletes,
The conical morels and woodsy chanterelles,
The fragrant matsutakes and purple-tipped corals;
But best of all, the kingdom's prize,
Its cap, tan and fleshy and kidskin smooth—
Boletus edulis, the king itself!
Of these and where they grow,
The bloody, bawdy villain blabs
And blabs and blabs in tavern and in church,
In public squares, piazzas, and malls,
To anyone curious to know where
In the vast Northwest my mushrooms grow.
"Go," he says, "to such a place at such a season.
Here is a map, follow the arrows, note
Where the power line stretches across the hills,
And there you are where boletes grow,
So many and of such a giant size, they seem
Like stepping stones to the heaven
Of which all mushroom hunters dream."
So blabs the bloody, bawdy villain,
The prim, bespectacled mycologist.
And what was once my Sacred Grove, where I
Alone, and when the sun is right, my shadow,

Hunted and stalked the fungoid quarry,
And brought it home to enrich a sauce,
Or crown a steak, or move a loving wife
To incorporate acts of love—that Sacred Grove,
Once mine, is mine no more. It has become—
A ravaged, desecrated common, a stomping ground
For mincing nincompoops who hunt by the book.

He now fired a vile Italian stogie to purge the air of the stench of poachers. "Come along," he said, "let's try our luck on yonder hill. And if I find that poaching ruffian, I'll feed fat the ancient grudge I bear him. Cursed be my breed if I forgive him. By the way, have you ever had polenta with rabbit smothered with boletes?"

And without waiting for an answer he said, "We will have it this evening." And we did. Now you who read this shall have the recipe, the gift of a man whose vice on a mushroom hunt is balanced by his virtue in the parlor.

The polenta itself is a substitute for bread. It is made with coarsely ground yellow cornmeal cooked in boiling, salted water. In certain regions of Italy north of Rome, it is the bread substitute of the poor who cannot afford wheat bread. Eaten with nothing else and as a steady diet, it is a curse. Eaten occasionally and with quality accompaniments, it is a culinary triumph. Therefore, when it is listed on the home or restaurant menu, it is always as polenta *with* something or other; and it is that something or other that gives the dish status among Italy's *buongustai*, people of superior taste in edibles and potables.

However, when I was a boy in Italy, the poor could rarely afford to eat anything with polenta that was needed to make it, let us say, exceptionally palatable. When we could go to the swamps and catch frogs and then cook them in a rich tomato sauce aromatized with pennyroyal (*Mentha pulegium*), a polenta dinner was a feast. Less so and more expensive was polenta with *baccalá*, sun-dried and salted cod, cooked in a tomato sauce with plenty of leeks. Normally, however, we ate it, much too often, with such indifferent accompaniments as onions, turnip greens, ripe figs, a bit of Parmesan cheese, and broiled pilchards. These came pressed in barrels in a circular pattern—ugly, foul, putrefied little creatures from the Mediterranean.

In America, of course, it has been otherwise. When the polenta is well made with coarsely ground cornmeal so that it is granular rather than gummy, like a good baking potato, and when it is served with rabbit, fresh fish, game birds, or a combination of chicken and Italian sausage, then it becomes a dinner such as a peasant would serve if he could afford it.

The polenta itself is easily made. Here is an approximate recipe for four: A quart and a half of water and a pound and a half of cornmeal. Double the amount of both for eight people; but have plenty of cornmeal on hand. Bring the water to a boil, salt to taste, and, stirring briskly with a large wooden spoon, add half of the cornmeal. The continuous stirring is necessary to prevent lumps from forming. When it begins to thicken, add the rest of the meal in driblets and continue the stirring. (The kettle of adequate size should be of cast iron or heavy aluminum.)

The end product should be so thick and dense that a spoonful of it will hold its shape. Hence the need to add the cornmeal in driblets, giving it plenty of time to increase the thickness until the proper degree of density is achieved. This, of course, occurs slowly; so don't hurry the addition of the meal. Continue the stirring and cooking over low heat for about twenty minutes after the proper density has been achieved. (Total cooking time is about forty-five minutes.)

Now increase the heat and, with a spatula, shape the surface of the polenta into a slight dome; then, with lightning speed, turn the kettle upside down onto a smooth surface such as a mincing board. The steam generated by the increased heat will disengage the polenta from the bottom of the kettle. In a few minutes it will set so that it may be sliced.

Cut the rabbit in small pieces. Dust them with flour and brown them on both sides in enough olive oil to drench the bottom of the skillet. Salt and pepper to taste. When nicely browned, add a cup of dry vermouth or white wine acidulated with the juice of half a lemon. Increase the heat and stir until the wine is partly evaporated. Remove the pieces with a slotted spoon.

Mince finely half a medium onion, the leafy end of a rib of celery, enough carrot to make a heaping tablespoon, and four cloves of garlic, and slice thinly half a pound of mushrooms. Sauté these in the same skillet, adding a bit more oil if necessary, over low heat to avoid scorching. Stir into this mixture a heaping tablespoon of minced parsley and a level tablespoon of fresh thyme, or half a tablespoon of the dry. Then add a small tin of tomato sauce. To a cup and a half of stock, add a couple of squirts of Tabasco, a dash of allspice, and one of nutmeg. Stir in a teaspoon of arrowroot and add to the sautéed ingredients. The result will be a dense but fluid sauce.

Place the rabbit pieces in a baking dish and pour the sauce over them. Clamp on the lid and bake in a 350-degree oven for about forty-five minutes. As required, add enough stock or wine to keep the quantity of the sauce constant. Needless to say, the rabbit should be prepared so that it is in the oven while the polenta is being made. Or it may be prepared some time before.

Serve it thus: Arrange two thin slices of the polenta on each plate. Scatter over them small chunks of tuma cheese, cover them with two other thin slices, and pour over them the rabbit with plenty of sauce.

—*Seattle Weekly*

MUSHROOMS

AUTUMN. THE MELANCHOLY days are here again, the saddest of the year, days of the fall of leaf, reminder of one's mortality. So much for the poet. It is also the season of the apple, the pear, the grape, the fig, and the mushroom.

Gathering wild mushrooms is a relatively new experience for many Americans, a phase of our coming of age gastronomically. We do not yet pursue it with the greed and zest and folkloristic superstitions that attended the hunt among the peasants of my native Italy. For them, the wild mushroom was not hunted to grace a steak or to raise the gastronomic level of a full dinner plate: they had neither. It was used to make stale, coarse bread more palatable, and to sell when pennies were needed to buy what could not be grown on the land.

Hence the avidity, the competition that attended the hunt, and the superstitious beliefs that were thought to assure its success. One had to go to the forest at the crack of dawn, make the sign of the cross before entering the mushroom patch, wear a garment inside out, and carry a probing stick that had acquired the virtue of a magic wand, and a tote bag, usually an old pillowcase, that had never been washed. The mushroom hunter then drank a glass of wine and began the hunt.

The proverbial sanction required it: *Non ti mettere in cammino se la bocca non sa di vino*—never venture forth on anything of consequence without the taste of wine in your mouth. And what could possibly be of more consequence than the search for mushrooms?

Success in the hunt was always attributed to these proverbial and superstitious preparations. When it failed, when there were telltale traces in the area that others had been there, the appropriate response was, *Ci sono bell' e stati!*—others have been happily here before us. Happily, because happiness is coming upon a host of mushrooms, especially what we call *Boletus edulis* —the King. Unfortunately for us, theirs was the happiness this time. Better luck for us next time. Such was the traditional, humane lament. Someone less humane might simply have uttered a curse: "Damn the ruffian who beat us to the patch!"

The patch, the grove, the limited area where one found mushrooms year after year, came to be regarded as one's own. Leading others to it, or even indicating in what general direction it lay, was simply out of the question. Such exclusive right to the patch, however, was invariably illusory, for sooner or later some roving hunter would find it.

How characteristically different is the American's orientation toward the mushroom hunt. No traditions, no superstitions, no avidity, no competition, no exclusive claim to the patch. Americans dress well for the woods, wicker basket in hand with a sandwich, a thermos of coffee, a mushroom book. If they find a patch, they share it with friends, and, inevitably, a mycological society is organized, officers elected, membership fees set, periodic meetings arranged. The mushroom hunt becomes a cooperative outing; it's the American, the democratic way, the way of people for whom the mushroom is not so much a food as a luxury.

May I now suggest two ways of preparing chanterelles? Clean them with a soft brush—mushrooms should never be washed. Slice them and put them in a skillet with nothing added. These mushrooms contain considerable water. Simmer them until it has all been evaporated. Then add the necessary olive oil and butter and a mince of parsley, garlic, and shallots. Salt and pepper to taste, and sauté them over medium heat to avoid burning. When they are about done, sprinkle a bit of arrowroot over them, stir thoroughly, and add half a cup of dry vermouth. The result will be a dense but fluid sauce.

I have omitted from the mince an herb that you are not likely to have. The Italian name is *nepitella*, the appropriate aromatic in mushroom cookery. When one buys wild mushrooms there, a few sprigs of nepitella are usually included. If one may trust the Italian-English dictionary, the English name is calamint, one of the several aromatic plants of the genus *Satureja*. I found it in an Italian produce market in San Francisco, some thirty years ago. Since it reseeds itself, it crops up in various places in my garden, and when I cook mushrooms, I always add a dozen or so leaves to the mince. Search for nepitella until you find it. It is worth the effort, for this aromatic is to mushroom cookery what dill is to pickles.

Another way to prepare chanterelles is to remove the stems, dip the caps in a light egg and flour batter, and fry them in a small amount of olive or other oil until they are nicely browned on both sides. Salt and pepper to taste, add a few drops of lemon juice, and you will be happy with the result. For this method, it is best to use the small, firm chanterelles. Boletes, also, are best prepared in this way.

Enjoy the search for the herb, good luck, and *buon appetito.*

—Seattle Weekly

ZUCCHINI

IT MAY BE that there is a collective uncertainty about what zucchini are and the preferred ways to cook them. Since they are of Italian origin and I have eaten them regularly for eighty years, I will share with you what I have learned. Zucchini are no more a proper subject for humor than the several other members of the Cucurbitaceae (the large botanical family to which they belong), such as melons, cucumbers, pumpkins, gourds, and squash.

The Italian word for pumpkin and squash is *zucca*; and zucchini is the plural of the diminutive and masculine *zucchino*. When the feminine form is used, as it sometimes is, the word becomes *zucchina* in the singular, *zucchine* in the plural. Whatever the gender, the suffix indicates that the zucca is tiny in its herbaceous integrity, and eaten in its entirety. In quantitatively oriented America, this needs special emphasis. Zucchini that are as large as or larger than cucumbers are, for most purposes, past their prime. The educated palate requires that they be about four inches long, an inch or less in diameter, and the flower at the tip virginal and intact.

There is a morphological reason for this. The edible and

choice parts of the zucchino are the green rind and the sort of embryonic pulp inside that bears the numerous seeds when fully developed. As the zucchino grows toward maturity, the size and shape of a large watermelon, the rind becomes tough, and the pulp, bland and of only slight nutritive value, increases in bulk. People who grow their own should harvest them before this stage. Others must shop wisely and select the smallest zucchini available. If they are too large, cut them longitudinally in quarters, and slice off the seedy part of the pulp.

The Italian dictionary, as part of the definition of zucchini, states the two ways they are generally prepared for the table: First, sliced, boiled *al dente*, and served with a condiment of olive oil, salt, and pepper (to which I would add a spray of lemon juice). The other, and tastier, of the two ways is thus: slice them, dust them with flour, drench them in beaten egg, and fry them in just enough oil, over moderate heat, to a golden brown on both sides. When they are small and the bloom is sound, the zucchini should be sliced lengthwise together with the bloom. When the slicing is done properly and the zucchini is not overcooked, the reward is a delicious morsel.

People who grow their own should also know that the zucchini vine produces many sterile flowers growing on long stems, rather than at the end of the zucchino. These flowers, with the bitter stamen removed and fried as described above, are a delicacy worthy of note in any transcendental gastronomy.

Zucchini, cut lengthwise in narrow strips, are often boiled or steamed with green beans and served with melted butter or olive oil. Since the zucchini cook more quickly, they should be added when the beans are nearly done. Green onions and zucchini coarsely chopped make an excellent frittata. They are also indispensable in a classic minestrone. One may also dine elegantly with zucchini, peppers, and tomatoes stuffed with a combination of ground meat, aromatics, and grated cheese. When thus used, select the larger ones, about the size of cucumbers. Cut them lengthwise, scoop out the pulp, sprinkle with salt and pepper, and press the cooked filling in the cavity. Arrange them in a baking dish and add a bit of water and tomato juice, enough to cover the bottom. Bake in a 350-degree preheated oven just long enough to cook the vegetable shell.

So much for the ubiquitous zucchini. Grow your own, if you have a kitchen garden, and be assured of their ubiquity. A vine, well established and fertilized, will bear fruit well into the autumn season.

—Seattle Weekly

RISOTTO

O<small>N A MONDAY</small> in March, at seven minutes past two P.M., there was a power outage in our area. Have you ever had an outage, a phenomenon defined by the dictionary as a "temporary suspension of operation, especially of electric power"? If not, don't feel neglected: bide your time, and the age of technology will spring one on you when you least expect it. You may be operating your vacuum cleaner, or lawn edger, or Cuisinart, and suddenly the operation ceases. That's an outage. You may have bread or a cake in the oven, and the temporary failure leaves you stunned and wondering how long it will last.

Or the visitation may occur, as it did to us, on a day you are making preliminary preparations for a six-thirty dinner party. Two hours later, a call to City Light tells you the crew is trying to locate the cause. At six, you are informed that they are still trying. You call the guests and tell them dinner will be delayed because of the outage. Do they mind waiting until technology overcomes technology's failure? Assured that they do not mind, you tell them you will call when the power is restored. At seven, City Light tells you the power may return within two hours.

Candles are lit. The fire glows in the grate. You ask the guests to come and wait out the outage with you. There is bread and cheese to nibble and wine to sip.

They come, and at eight what was supposed to be temporary threatens to be permanent. Postpone the dinner? No way! Everyone is enjoying the unique experience. You serve the salad of spring-growth chicory with a dressing of oil, lemon, minced garlic, and a pinch of curry, freshly baked bread, and a bottle of Robert Mondavi Chardonnay Reserve. The tempo of gaiety accelerates and—to hell with the outage.

And, says one of the guests, your stove is dead, we have a live one. I can have it here in ten mlnutes. At nine, a very efficient Coleman stove is set up in the living room, and a seafood risotto, the ingredients for which were prepared earlier, is simmering on one of the burners. If you've never had such a risotto, add this to your culinary repertoire.

Mince and, in olive oil and butter, sauté an onion, half a rib of celery, half a carrot, and some parsley, using a large saucepan. Stir in a cup and a half of rice over high heat. Do this briskly until rice and flavoring agents are thoroughly mixed. Then add a glass of dry vermouth and stir until it has been completely absorbed by the rice. Have ready a hot fish broth enriched by clam juice. Add it in small amounts from time to time, and keep stirring over low heat. When the broth has been absorbed, add some more and continue this until the rice is done. (For piquancy, if desired, add two squirts of Tabasco to the broth.) When the rice is completely cooked, stir in raw clams, some shrimp or prawns cut in small pieces, and squid similarly cut, including the tentacles. Serve hot, overspread with finely minced Italian parsley.

Don't sprinkle Parmesan or other grated cheese on seafood risotto—unless you must have it.

At our Monday night dinner, the risotto was served as a first course. The main course was to have been a pork leg roast, laved with minced garlic, sage, olive oil, and a sprinkling of wine vinegar, done on an electric rotisserie using reflected heat from the fireplace. That, of course, could not be done, so the roast was sliced into thin steaks and cooked in a skillet on the Coleman. At ten, while we were eating the first course by candlelight, the lights came on as silently as they had gone off. Such are the marvels of technology.

—Seattle Weekly

TOMATOES

AUTUMN! SEASON OF mists and mellow fruitfulness, a time when a proper regard for one's belly and a sound domestic economy require the preservation of the season's produce. In my Italian peasant family, neither freezing nor canning was available to us. Sun and salt were our preserving agents. We would slice firm ripe tomatoes, dry them in the sun for two or three days, salt them, and pack them in olive oil in small containers to use principally as a flavoring ingredient in our cuisine. We also made a concentrated tomato paste called *conserva*, and when, in America, we had learned to preserve by canning, we made a tomato sauce unequaled in flavor by the commercial product. For those of you who are eager to add these to the resources of your kitchen, I shall give an account of the entire process for making both the sauce and the conserva.

First the sauce. You will need thoroughly ripe tomatoes, thyme, parsley, celery leaves, basil, and salt. My recipe suggests proportions for these ingredients, but having mastered these, you may want to vary them quantitatively. You may also experiment with an herb combination other than the above.

Crush eight pounds of tomatoes into a kettle of adequate capacity. Add a tablespoon of fresh thyme leaves and, in roughly equal parts, enough of the other three herbs so that when compacted in the hands they form a ball about the size of a large orange. These will give the sauce the desired flavor. Bring it to a rolling boil, stirring as necessary to prevent the solids from burning in the bottom of the kettle. Add salt to taste, reduce the heat, and let the compound simmer for about an hour and a half. The simmering evaporates some of the liquid, imparts the flavor of the herbs to the emerging sauce, and permeates the kitchen and adjoining rooms with an aroma that will provoke anticipatory salivation. Stir now and then to prevent sticking and to help evaporate the watery liquid. For a thick sauce simmer for about an hour and a half.

Using a large colander, drain off the free-run liquid into a bowl without pressing. To remove skins, seeds, and the fibrous portion of the herbs, press the residual solids in a food mill or other similar utensil. Do this thoroughly in order to extract all the pulp. The result will be a dense but fluid tomato sauce. The free-run, pleasantly flavored juice may be drunk, or preserved to flavor stock and vegetable soups.

To make conserva (tomato paste), add more salt to the thick sauce as a preservative, spread it in a shallow pan, screen it against flies, and put it in the sun. Stir it as necessary to expose the moist underside to the sun. In two or three days, if the temperature has been in the high seventies or above, the color will be a dark burgundy, and the concentrate will be dense enough to shape with the hands, but first oil your hands to prevent sticking, and then shape into a ball or patty. Press this into a sterilized jar, screw on the band, and store in the refrigerator. That will be your vintage conserva for the year. The salt and the oil will prevent spoiling.

If the necessary sun to make conserva is lacking, process the thick sauce in this way: Bring it to a soft boil, pour it into scalding hot, half-pint jars filled to the brim, put on the hot self-sealing lid, and screw on the band. No further processing is necessary. This will be your year's supply of tomato sauce. Having followed these directions with a gratifying sense of creative labor, you will have on hand a flavoring agent of incomparable quality, not even remotely approximated by the commercial varieties of tomato paste and sauce. If possible, it is advisable to have on hand both the conserva and the sauce. Use the one or the other in recipes that require the tomato flavor.

In using them remember that they are highly flavored concentrates, the conserva more than the sauce, and should be used sparingly. A third of a teaspoon of conserva, diluted with a bit of hot stock, will do wonders to the family stew, a mushroom sauce for steak, a beef or chicken broth. A tablespoon of the less concentrated sauce will yield the same result. When I was a boy in Italy, Mother spread a thin layer of conserva on bread of poor quality to make it more palatable.

The reason for processing the tomato sauce in half-pint jars is that, as a flavoring agent, it is always used in small quantities. What is left in the jar should be covered with oil; then it can be kept in the refrigerator indefinitely. However, in using it for other sauces, such as the classic meat sauce for one pound of pasta, you will need the entire half-pint.

For a sauce of rare excellence, add this to your culinary achievements: In a blend of butter and olive oil, as much of each as suits your taste, mince five cloves of garlic, and six fillets of anchovy cut in small pieces. Sauté these until the garlic turns a light brown, then add the half-pint of sauce. Stir with a fork to homogenize the whole, add a squirt of Tabasco and as much lemon pepper as you like. Simmer for only a few minutes. The condiment is ample for one pound of pasta. Sprinkle each serving with grated Parmesan cheese.

—*Seattle Weekly*

RUMINATIONS

RUMINATION OF AN OCTOGENARIAN

*[A speech to students at the
University of Washington, November 1987]*

Do I QUALIFY as such or am I an impostor? Banish the thought! Note the scant gray hair, the bushy eyebrows flecked with white, the parentheses which enclose the nose and mouth, the patriarchal sobriety, the conventional garment. I am indeed well into what are euphemistically called the Golden Years, a Retiree, a Senior Citizen, an Emeritus, which is another euphemism for a professor put to pasture in order to make room in the dens of learning for the young lions.

The poet Eliot said of the poet Wordsworth that in youth he wrote great lyrical ballads; and that in old age he merely ruminated. Having achieved the Golden Years, willy-nilly, and having failed to write great lyrics, I have come here to ruminate so that you, expecting I know not what, may witness an act of rumination in the flesh. An act! A rare privilege for a well-aged roguish actor!

The word "ruminate" derives from the Latin *rumen*, which is the first division of the stomach of a ruminant; and a ruminant is a horned, four-footed creature that chews its cud. The intake is given a preliminary mastication, then is sent to the rumen, whence it is regurgitated, chewed again, and sent on its way down the alimentary canal. By considerable poetic license, the scene of action has been transferred from the belly to the mind, the physical has become metaphysical, and the verb "to ruminate," as here used, means to reflect, to meditate, to ponder. I lack the salient attributes of the ruminant: the four feet, the knack of re-gurgitation, the horns. Darwin accounts for the lack of the first two; and my wife's unquestioned fidelity accounts for a brow without horns. But in compensation for these deficiencies, I have had several decades of experience in chewing, ingesting, and di-gesting the succulent American cud; and it is certain end results of this experience that I propose to share with you. It is a most congenial task, undertaken with confidence and serenity; for these constitute the virtue in one whom a great deal of good fortune has enabled to achieve the Golden Years with no major regrets. Unlike Macbeth, I have not lived long enough; nor has my way of life fallen into the sere, the yellow leaf. I have lived and loved and labored; and since my goals, revised from time to time as cir-cumstances required, were ever modest, I have achieved them with relative ease. There is work yet to do; the hands are still capable; the mind unimpaired; the sap still flows. Don't urge me to be more precise about these equivocations!

However, I must tell you that I once wrote a poem, and that during the past thirty years I have established myself as an amateur historian of the Italian immigrant. The poem, in the manner of Wordsworth's *Michael*, was a sophomoric outburst of ill-digested piety. It was properly forgotten as soon as it was published. But my historical works have been widely read and intelligently reviewed. For the first I was rewarded with a Guggenheim Fellowship. A chapter of the second was published in translation in Italy. The third was translated into Spanish and into the several languages of India; and it was distributed abroad in a paperback edition by the State Department. Collectively, these are my credentials as a ruminating octogenarian.

There is a ruminating way of coming to terms with the golden years, an Irish way stated thus:

When you are old and gray and full of sleep,
And nodding by the fire, take down this book,
And slowly read, and dream of the soft look
Your eyes had once, and of their shadows deep;

How many loved your moments of glad grace,
And loved your beauty with love false or true
But one man loved the pilgrim soul in you,
And loved the sorrows of your changing face;

And bending down beside the glowing bars,
Murmur, a little sadly, how Love fled
And paced upon the mountains overhead
And hid his face amid a crowd of stars.

Proceeding from the Irish to the Anglo-Saxon mode of rumination—remember the Bard of Stratford-on-Avon. In his last play, *The Tempest*, he stated that we are "such stuff as dreams are made on, and our little life is rounded with a sleep." That is not my mode. Rounded with a sleep? Our *little* life rounded with a sleep?

> To die, to sleep;
> To sleep: perchance to dream: ay, there's the rub;
> For in that sleep of death what dreams may come
> When we have shuffled off this mortal coil,
> Must give us pause. There's the respect
> That makes calamity of so long life;
> For who would bear the whips and scorns of time,
> The oppressor's wrong, the proud man's contumely,
> The pangs of dispriz'd love, the law's delay,
> . . . When he himself might his quietus make
> With a bare bodkin? Who would fardels bear,
> To grunt and sweat under a weary life,
> But that the dread of something after death,
> The undiscover'd country from whose bourn
> No traveller returns, puzzles the will,
> And makes us rather bear those ills we have,
> Than fly to others that we know not of?

No, no, no! That is not my mode of rumination. It is but a playful way, a rogue and peasant slave's way, of returning to the classroom for a passing salute to Hamlet without even an attempt to solve the riddle of the Prince of Denmark. And now that I have indulged myself, let's get on with the rumination. There is no dread in me of what may be in the undiscovered country from whose bourn no traveler returns. That sort of preoccupation is pure Anglo-Saxon, pure Bunyan. I prefer the mode of the Irish poet. Focus on life; cherish the memories which record its notable moments. Ruminate, meditate, ponder. Remember when you are old and gray and full of sleep and nodding by the fire. Remember how love fled and paced upon the mountains overhead and hid his face amid a crowd of stars. Remember the glory of that love and its brevity.

The greatest man in Italian letters went to and returned from the undiscovered country from whose bourn no traveler returns. In Hell he learned the meaning of eternal damnation, in purgatory the ways of purgation, and in Paradise, the Empyrean, with the aid of Beatrice, he got a glimpse of the Love that moves the sun and the other stars, *l'amor che move il sole e l'altre stelle*. I am not Dante, but when I courted *my* Beatrice, I knew no less than he, that I was transfigured by *l'amor che move il sole e l'altre stelle*. That was fifty-six years ago. We are now old and gray and we sleep well. Perhaps we are such stuff as dreams are made on; but our little life is not rounded by a sleep. She is of Irish and I of Italic descent.

My life as a ruminating octogenarian is rounded by certain memories, in the glow of which I pursue my diurnal agenda in my study, in the garden, in the kitchen, in the cellar. In my study I scourge my mind to keep it unimpaired; in the garden I grow herbage for the table. These photosynthesize, and their release of oxygen in the atmosphere adds to the salubrious ecology of View Ridge. My work in the kitchen is reflected in the weighty appearance of my Beatrice, whom the women of her club call a Renaissance Lady. In the cellar I make wine for the family to complement the bread I bake in the kitchen. Bread and wine!

Pane e vino! The one makes the heart strong; the other makes it glad. I also love, but with a far-ranging passion appropriate to a ruminating octogenarian, a passion purged of carnal appetite. What a pity!

First and foremost of the memories which give a transcendent glow to my crepuscular years is of the day my parents brought me to America. I was ten years of age and had completed the third grade in Italy. As a son of sharecropper peasants that would have been the end of my formal education. But the law in this state required that I should go to school until I was sixteen. Which I did. On January 4, 1914, not knowing one word of English, I began my study of the language in the first grade in McCleary, Grays Harbor County. A succession of affectionate, competent teachers taught me so well that in eight years I began my university studies. Where else in this best of all possible worlds could that have been possible? Surely not in Tuscan Italy!

Another of the various memories is of the day I got a first and fleeting glimpse of the Renaissance Lady. With twenty-twenty vision I saw her, and a voice from the region of the liver—which the Elizabethans thought was the seat of love—cried out with relentless urgency, "Sweep her into your orbit!" And now there are two daughters, a son, and myself on this swiftly tilting planet, whirling merrily in *her* orbit. (It is morning, Senlin says; and in the morning when the light drips through the shutters like the dew, I arise, I face the sunlight, and do the things my fathers used to do. Stars in the purple dusk above the rooftops pale in a saffron mist and seem to die; and I myself on a swiftly tilting planet, stand before the glass and tie my tie. Ho dear me! What a ruminating octogenarian can come up with!)

I remember the time when I was in the elementary grades. The discrimination against the Italians was brutal. As one of its victims, in order to escape the abuse by my young classmates, I was tempted to quicken the process of Americanization by changing my name to Pennington and my diet from pasta al pesto to mashed potatoes and gravy. On the advice of my fourth-grade teacher, I resisted the temptation. "You are the only bilingual in the entire school, the faculty included," she said. "You are the scion of a great civilization. You can become a good American without forsaking your native heritage. Add to your knowledge of the language and learn more about your native land." I did. And thereafter I defied the proud man's contumely by abusing my vulgar peers in good Italian as they had abused me in bad English. *Brutti, maleducati schifosi.* You ugly, ill-bred wretches! Such were my verbal, unanswered thrusts, delivered with fiendish glee.

What though the field be lost! All is not lost, the indomitable will and study of revenge! Forgive my erstwhile Satanic Pride! I was a cocky, dark-eyed kid testing my mettle in the New World. The long-range results of my teacher's advice were many. During the next decades I chewed with unabated hunger the succulent American cud, what Walt Whitman called Fecund America!

> Thou envy of the globe! thou miracle!
> Thou, bathed, choked, swimming in plenty,
> Thou lucky mistress of the tranquil barns . . .
> Thou mental, moral orb . . . !

The regurgitations thereof were the stuff of other memories, other vanities, and nine books. The ninth, *The American Dream*, is my best, perhaps my testament. A radio station in New York City will broadcast a telefonic interview with me on the book on November 17. Another vanity to add to my other vanities. This I say with as much humility as the cocky kid now old and gray and ruminating can muster.

I am done, though not quite done. Let me indulge myself once more. Dante and Shakespeare divided the world of poetry between them; such was the judgment of T. S. Eliot. The one forged the Italian language, the other perfected the English. Both have given me all the spiritual sustenance I could digest. On two near-tragic moments in my life I turned to them for solace. Once, forty years ago, when a committee of the legislature, organized to investigate radical activities, threatened my career. Certain that I had done no wrong, as I stood defenseless before its chairman, who was armed with absolute power, I thought of Shakespeare's brief profile of such as he: "Man, proud man, drest in a little brief authority, most ignorant of what he's most assur'd, his glassy essence, like an angry ape, plays such fantastic tricks before high heaven, as make the angels weep." There was solace in that. Certain that I had done no wrong! Soon thereafter I was given a medal and a cash award by Freedom Foundation in Valley Forge for having made a significant contribution to a better understanding of the American Way of Life. The chairman of the committee, as a candidate for a seat in Congress from his district, was defeated. There was solace in that.

The other near-tragic moment was the result of my folly. On a mushroom hunt with my wife, son Brent, and Greg Markov in the Cascades, I foolishly separated myself from them and became lost. The weather was foul, rain and snow. From noon to dusk I sought my way out in vain. Waiting for the dawn, drenched to the bone, I leaned against a tree for eight hours. At two-thirty in the morning, my life in jeopardy, I thought of Dante: *Nel mezzo del cammin di nostra vita, mi ritrovai per una selva oscura, ché la diritta via era smarrita.* Midway in our life's journey I went astray from the straight road and lodged in a dark forest. These verses I addressed to what stars were visible. Then the miracle: two bloodhounds. And here I am!

Once more I am done, though not quite done. Among the memories in the glow of which I pursue my diurnal agenda, there is one most notable that I must mention before I take my leave. It is of the time I did what had never been done before in a university community in America: I invited a dean and the president of the university to our home for dinner. Dinner? Just plain dinner for the hierarchs of a great university? Remember who I am: a master of the culinary art celebrated as far away as Australia. Accordingly, what I prepared, after sustained ruminations on what would be appropriate, was the very prototype of transcendental gastronomy. Do these evocative phrases challenge your imagination? Make you just a wee bit envious?

There were vintage wines, of course. Photosynthesizing herbage from the garden, naturally; home-baked bread to be sure. And the main course, the pièce de résistance? The first division of the stomach of a ruminant, which the vulgar may call tripe. Has anyone in the American university community ever done this? Does anyone want the recipe? And with this, the ruminating octogenarian takes his leave.

PELLE'S FOLLY

At about two in the morning on October 8, 1982, having nothing more appropriate to do, I was reciting the opening verses of Dante's *Divina Commedia*:

> *Nel mezzo del cammin di nostra vita*
> *mi ritrovai per una selva oscura,*
> *ché la diritta via era smarrita.*
>
> *Ahi quanto a dir era è cosa dura*
> *esta selva selvaggia e aspra e forte*
> *che nel pensier rinova la paura!*
>
> (In the middle of the journey of our life,
> having strayed from the straight path,
> I found myself in a dark wood.
> Ah! how hard a thing it is to tell
> what a wild and rough and stubborn wood this was,
> which in my very thought renews the fear.)

Dante then states that in the early morning hours, when he surveyed more closely the place where he had arrived, he noticed that he was at the foot of a hill, its shoulders bathed in light; but when he tried to climb toward those "sweetest rays," whose sight lessened his fear, a nimble leopard stood in his way.

These verses, of course, are all symbol and allegory. Dante was in the Dark Wood of Error, where he had spent hours of great misery and from which he must safely emerge. At the time I recited them, however, every word described what was for me a grim reality—a dark forest from which I must emerge or, possibly, perish in the attempt. There was a bitter irony in the fact that I was actually living through a misadventure such as one might read about in some romance or epic.

Note the striking similarity between what the poet imagined and my own predicament: Two o'clock in the morning, I was in the foothills of the Cascades in the Stampede Pass region, on a road parallel to a power line. Having searched for a way out of the forest after a mushroom hunt, I had made some wrong turns and after walking for five hours I had arrived there at about six-thirty in the evening. Unable to go farther because of the darkness, I had stopped there to wait for the dawn.

Still thinking of the poet, I surveyed the near and distant landscape in order to determine what course I should pursue in the morning. Beyond the clearing that was the right-of-way for the power line was a dense wood. At its edge, a few hundred feet away, I saw in the fading twilight an animal, partially hidden, slinking through the shrubbery in a course parallel to the power line. Was it a deer? Dante's leopard in the shape of a cougar? Why on that course? Why did it not slink away from me and into the woods?

While thus preoccupied and determined not to yield to fear, I heard a most reassuring noise: the roar of trucks on a distant highway. In the gathering darkness, I was able to see the road on the flank of a steep, wooded hill, to the right of the spot on which I stood, and in the general direction I had been traveling when I stopped for the night. At brief intervals I could see the flicker of moving lights through the partial clearings on the flank of the hill: Dante's "sweetest rays." Somehow, I must get to that highway. As the crow flies, it seemed less than a mile away. Assuming that the "leopard" would not stay my way, in an hour or so in the morning I would be "out of the woods." Since it was now six-thirty, I braced myself for a long night's vigil; but more on this later.

I must now go back in time several hours and relate how I happened to stray from the straight path and follow others that led to the grim reality described above, and what happened thereafter. I shall always remember what I am about to relate as Pellegrini's Folly, an aberration, however, that was luckily balanced by what remained in me of vintage Pellegrini. The story is unavoidably subjective and personal, written at the request of my editor, both for its intrinsic merit as the account of a frightening experience, and for what there may be in it by way of a warning to mushroom hunters and others who may lose their way in the wilderness.

At ten o'clock in the morning, October 7, my wife, our son Brent, Gregory Markov, and I entered what we called "our mushroom patch" in the hills on the way to Stampede Pass. We had parked our car by a stream about a quarter of a mile behind us and only a short distance from the Stampede Pass road, which is much used by logging trucks, the Forest Service, and Kittitas County vehicles. Our plan was to hunt mushrooms for a couple of hours and then return to the car to eat our lunch. It was raining. At a slightly higher elevation it was snowing. But the mushrooms were prime and plentiful. The area of densely wooded patch was about three-quarters of a square mile. I knew it well since I had been there many times in years past with fellow hunters other than members of my family.

It had always been our planned strategy to keep in touch with each other by whistling or calling. Since on this occasion I was the oldest in the group and the most experienced in the area, I should have insisted that we return to the car together when we were through mushrooming. This I foolishly failed to do. In the excitement of the hunt I became separated from the others. When they had all the mushrooms they could carry, they returned to the car, according to plan. It was perfectly natural for them to assume that I had either preceded them or would soon follow; I was, in a sense, their guide. There was no reason for them to assume otherwise.

However, with the insatiable greed of my breed of mushroom hunters, and with prime boletes beckoning me in various directions, I plunged deeper and deeper into the forest. By the time my water bucket was filled with the finest boletes I have ever gathered, I had wandered away from the familiar area. When I finally emerged from the forest and onto one of the many paths that crisscross that wilderness, I knew not which way to turn. I checked the time. It was one-thirty and still raining. But instead of waiting there, I compounded my folly by moving on, confident that I would find my way. I should have known—being old and wise—that Brent and Gregory would return to the area to search for me, which, I learned later, they did, for two hours until four-thirty in the afternoon. Had I remained there and hollered occasionally, they would certainly have found me.

But I moved on. My psyche began to trick me. What was real became unreal. I was not lost. It never occurred to me that I was lost. The path led to a road, which I followed without even pausing to choose a direction. Wet to the bone, carrying the heavy bucket with ease, I walked briskly, firm in the illusion that every step brought me closer to my wife and son and Gregory, who must certainly be deep in worry about me. Anyone observing me would have seen a seventy-nine-year-old man who knew where he was going and was determined to get there quickly.

For the next three hours, with undiminished confidence and unabated energy, in a steady drizzle, I walked along various roads until I came to a power line. There I climbed an upthrust of granite supporting one of its steel towers and scanned the horizons to see if I could spot a familiar landmark. Looking straight ahead along the power line's right-of-way in the direction I had been walking, I saw a vertical narrow clearing on a distant hillside up from the Stampede Pass road, near where the car was parked. Certain that I was now on target, with the distance to the clearing seeming rather close, and still firm in the illusion that I was not lost, I walked toward it with renewed energy. I was not tired, and though drenched to the bone, I was not cold. The clothing I was wearing, sweats under corduroy trousers, a wool shirt, a light jacket, and rain gear, prevented the escape of the body heat generated by vigorous walking.

The terrain under the power line—grassy, level, spotted with shrubbery—as seen from the elevation from which I had surveyed it, seemed easy to traverse. But it proved to be otherwise. When I had walked about half a mile, I came to what I shall call the Bog of Despair, a swamp dotted with watery chuckholes hidden in the grass. Beyond it, partially hidden by the shrubbery on its near bank, was a stream; and beyond the stream was the slightly higher elevation, which I had to reach.

Had I finally come upon my Nemesis, the avenger of my folly? Somehow I must cross the stream. (I later learned that it was a tributary of the Yakima River.) To reach its near bank was difficult. Issuing from it were numerous swirling rivulets, and the tangled shrubbery was dense. I plunged into one up to my crotch and felt a slight twist in my left ankle. The right foot was so mired in the muck that in extracting it, I was afraid I might lose one of the cleated football shoes I was wearing. But I made it to the stream's edge. The water was deep, perhaps up to my breast in midstream, and the current was swift. Fortunately, there was a log across it, with its underside in the water, a short way upstream. Having reached it, I held on to it with my left hand; and lifting the bucket of mushrooms above the water with my right hand, I began taking the few steps that would deliver me from the Bog of Despair.

A couple of yards from the opposite bank, the water was deeper, perhaps above my head. Without any reluctance whatever, it being in the very nature of things the proper thing to do, I consigned the bucket of mushrooms to the current, and swam the few strokes necessary to reach the bank. Holding firmly onto branches that overhung it, I pulled myself out of the water. With a sustained sigh of relief, I sat for a while to regain what composure was possible. Then I continued my journey toward that hillside clearing. It was not raining; I was not cold. When I had gone a few hundred yards, I came upon a well-defined road parallel to the power line. The going was easy and I was not tired. I checked the time to determine how much daylight remained. It was five-thirty.

Relieved of the weight of the mushrooms, I was now weighted down by a double burden: a terrible anxiety about my wife, my son, and Gregory—and about my own fate. I was certain that, by this time, they had begun to do whatever was necessary to summon aid. Gregory, a hiker, hunter, and mountain climber, would know the options available in dealing with such an emergency. My wife and son, I felt, would never leave the area until I was found, alive or dead. She must be convinced that I had suffered an accident, and I knew the agony that entailed. As for myself—had the surrender of the mushrooms, after having carried them so far, been the preamble to my total surrender? Were there world enough and time, as the poet said, I had the energy necessary to find my way out. I knew by now that the human organism has great reserves of resiliency and adaptability. Mine had certainly been put to the proof. But now it would soon be dark and further travel impossible.

Bearing these burdens with as much courage and confidence as I could bring to the challenge, I continued walking briskly until I arrived at my lodging for the night, described at the beginning of this story. It consisted of the shelter of two young fir trees growing side by side, about a foot apart and with intertwining branches close to the ground. Leaning against them, my cleated shoes firmed in the ground, I waited for the dawn. It would be a long wait, about twelve hours, plenty of time for me to review my predicament. Though drenched, I was not uncomfortably cold. In order to generate body heat, I must exercise, do some stationary jogging, spar with an imaginary opponent, rub my body.

I had no fear; but I had a clear, realistic perception of my total situation. There was some pain in my left ankle. I had had nothing to eat or drink since an early breakfast, and, although I had expended an enormous amount of energy, I was not hungry. Could I endure until morning? If so, would I then have enough energy to get to the highway? I recalled Darwin's theory of natural selection: the strong survive and the weak go to the wall. Would there be enough of vintage Pellegrini in me to place me among the Select? It had been snowing up in the hills in the morning. If the temperature should drop to the freezing point, would I die from hypothermia? If so, would death come gently, as in a sleep, without my being aware of it? Was I ready for death? Were my affairs in order? A ton of grapes would soon be delivered. Had I taught Brent enough about making wine? Would he find in my pocket the keys to my Mercedes?

Thus I reflected, and so marvelous is the adaptive capacity of the human organism that I had neither fear nor bodily weariness. This was a consoling discovery. For if I had been asked, while in the comfort of my home, whether I could endure all this with composure, without paralyzing despair, my answer would have been, "I doubt it." But the body in "good shape" cooperates marvelously with the mind that directs it. It is only to share this discovery with you that I have described in detail the bitter consequences of my folly. Insofar as it is within your means, tend your body and soul, and keep faith with Nature.

So it was that I leaned against those two trees from six-thirty in the evening until the early morning hours. My attitude was wholly secular. I thought of prayer, but only as an expedient available to those who believe in the certainty of Divine intervention. Bless them and their faith. I believed in the certainty that my wife and son, and the able and resourceful Gregory who knew precisely what to do, had by now summoned aid. It was two o'clock. Thinking that a helicopter might be somewhere above searching for me, I scanned the sky. All I saw was the moon playing peekaboo with the clouds. I began reciting an Italian poem which begins: "*Guarda che bianca luna*" (Behold, what a bright, white moon). Then once again, as I had several times before during my odyssey, I recited the opening verses of Dante's *Divina Commedia*. But this time I addressed the moon.

The recitation of poetry, while I am working in the garden or jogging on the quarter-mile track in the stadium, has become a habit. So on this occasion, inspired by the friendly, luminous moon, and to give the tedious, heavy hours some distracting content, I recited what poems, English and Italian, came to mind. With some difficulty, for the long hours of standing had severely taxed my legs, I stomped my way toward the tower of the power line, which here paralleled the road. And it was while I was leaning against it, listening to the hum of the wires above, that I began to wonder whether, in the morning, my legs would be able to carry me to the highway.

But it was destined that the doubt should never be resolved, for just then I heard a shrill whistle. Should I answer it? I decided against it, for fear that I might betray my presence to that beast, possibly a cougar, lurking at the edge of the forest. In a few minutes, I heard it again. It must be for me. Drawing upon what lung power I could muster, I managed a sustained yell. The reply was prompt: "PAA-lee, we are coming for you!" My name is Pelle, not Paylee; but no matter. I knew my odyssey was over. In a few minutes two bloodhounds were upon me, pawing and licking me with all the joy and excitement of a heroic mission accomplished, followed by six members of the Kittitas County Search and Rescue Team.

My wife and son and Gregory had done what I was certain they would do. After the sheriff had been contacted and the search party organized, Gregory Markov, remembering that I was wearing cleated shoes, had led the leader and the bloodhounds to the place where we had entered the mushroom patch. My wife had had the presence of mind to give the leader a pair of slippers I had brought along in case my feet should be wet after the hunt. The imprint of my cleated shoes was clearly visible on the wet ground. When the hounds had sniffed slippers and imprint, they led the search team directly to the place where I stood. The rest was jubilation. Devoted, efficient, humanitarian, those young men and women, led by a deputy sheriff, shall live in my gratitude for the rest of my days. When the leader of the search party reached me, he put his arms around what remained of vintage Pellegrini and said, "We love you."

—*Seattle Weekly*

ABOUT THE AUTHOR

ANGELO PELLEGRINI was born in Casabianca, Italy, and moved to McCleary, Washington, with his family in 1913. He received his Ph.D. in English from the University of Washington, where he is Professor Emeritus.

Pellegrini has been awarded a Freedom Foundation Medal and a Guggenheim Fellowship. He is the author of eight books, including *The Unprejudiced Palate* and *The Food Lover's Garden*.

He lives in Seattle with his wife, Virginia. They have three children and five grandchildren.

SCHUYLER INGLE is the co-author with Sharon Kramis of *Northwest Bounty: The Extraordinary Foods and Wonderful Cooking of the Pacific Northwest*. He is a freelance writer and editor in Seattle.

~~~~~